99 HEARTY SOUPS

99 HEARTY SOUPS

Deliciously sustaining recipes for rich and creamy chowders, comforting broths and tasty one-pot dishes, all shown step by step in 400 photographs

Debra Mayhew

HERMES HOUSE

This edition is published by Hermes House, an imprint of Anness Publishing Ltd, Hermes House,
88–89 Blackfriars Road, London SE1 8HA; tel. 020 7401 2077; fax 020 7633 9499

www.hermeshouse.com; www.annesspublishing.com

If you like the images in this book and would like to investigate using them for publishing, promotions or advertising,
please visit our website www.practicalpictures.com for more information.

Publisher: Joanna Lorenz
Managing Editor: Helen Sudell
Project Editor: Debra Mayhew and Helen Marsh
Recipes by: Catherine Atkinson, Alex Barker, Michelle Berriedale-Johnson, Angela Boggiano, Janet Brinkworth,
Carla Capalbo, Kit Chan, Jacqueline Clark, Maxine Clark, Frances Cleary, Carole Clements, Andi Clevely, Trish Davies,
Roz Denny, Patrizia Diemling, Matthew Drennan, Sarah Edmonds, Joanna Farrow, Rafi Fernandez, Christine France,
Sarah Gates, Shirley Gill, Rosamund Grant, Rebekah Hassan, Deh-Ta Hsiung, Shehzad Husain, Judy Jackson, Soheila Kimberley,
Masaki Ho, Elisabeth Lambert Ortiz, Ruby Le Bois, Gilly Love, Lesley Mackley, Norma MacMillan, Sue Maggs, Kathy Man,
Sallie Morris, Annie Nichols, Maggie Pannell, Katherine Richmond, Anne Sheasby, Jenny Stacey, Liz Trigg, Hilaire Walden,
Laura Washburn, Steven Wheeler, Kate Whiteman, Elizabeth Wolf-Cohen and Jeni Wright
Photographers: Karl Adamson, Edward Allwright, David Armstrong, Steve Baxter, James Duncan, John Freeman, Ian Garlick,
Michelle Garrett, Amanda Heywood, Janine Hosegood, David Jordan, William Lingwood, Patrick McLeary, Michael Michaels,
Thomas Odulate, Juliet Piddington and Peter Reilly
Designer: Bill Mason
Production Controller: Christine Ni

ETHICAL TRADING POLICY
At Anness Publishing we believe that business should be conducted in an ethical and ecologically sustainable way, with respect
for the environment and a proper regard to the replacement of the natural resources we employ.
As a publisher, we use a lot of wood pulp in high-quality paper for printing, and that wood commonly comes from spruce trees.
We are therefore currently growing more than 750,000 trees in three Scottish forest plantations: Berrymoss (130 hectares/
320 acres), West Touxhill (125 hectares/305 acres) and Deveron Forest (75 hectares/185 acres). The forests we manage contain
more than 3.5 times the number of trees employed each year in making paper for the books we manufacture.
Because of this ongoing ecological investment programme, you, as our customer, can have the pleasure and reassurance of
knowing that a tree is being cultivated on your behalf to naturally replace the materials used to make the book you are holding.
Our forestry programme is run in accordance with the UK Woodland Assurance Scheme (UKWAS) and will be certified by the
internationally recognized Forest Stewardship Council (FSC). The FSC is a non-government organization dedicated to promoting
responsible management of the world's forests. Certification ensures forests are managed in an environmentally sustainable and
socially responsible way. For further information about this scheme, go to www.annesspublishing.com/trees

A CIP catalogue record for this book is available from the British Library.

Previously published as *Hearty Soups*

NOTES
Bracketed terms are intended for American readers.
For all recipes, quantities are given in both metric and imperial measures and, where appropriate, in standard cups and spoons.
Follow one set of measures, but not a mixture, because they are not interchangeable.
Standard spoon and cup measures are level. 1 tsp = 5ml, 1 tbsp = 15ml, 1 cup = 250ml/8fl oz.
Australian standard tablespoons are 20ml. Australian readers should use 3 tsp in place of 1 tbsp for measuring small quantities.
American pints are 16fl oz/2 cups. American readers should use 20fl oz/2.5 cups in place of 1 pint when measuring liquids.
Electric oven temperatures in this book are for conventional ovens. When using a fan oven, the temperature will probably need to
be reduced by about 10–20°C/20–40°F. Since ovens vary, you should check with your manufacturer's instruction book for guidance.
Medium (US large) eggs are used unless otherwise stated.

Main front cover image shows Farmhouse Soup – for recipe, see page 101.

PUBLISHER'S NOTE
Although the advice and information in this book are believed to be accurate and true at the time of going to press, neither the
authors nor the publisher can accept any legal responsibility or liability for any errors or omissions that may have been made nor
for any inaccuracies nor for any loss, harm or injury that comes about from following instructions or advice in this book.

CONTENTS

Introduction

Nothing is so warming and comforting as a steaming bowl of filling home-made soup to stave off hunger, especially on a cold winter's evening. The wonderfully appetizing aroma is always especially welcoming.

All the recipes in this book are both nutritious and delicious – and many are substantial enough to provide an easy-to-make and satisfying meal in a bowl. Delicately flavoured soups, not normally associated with being "hearty" are also included. These would make a memorable first course for a formal or informal dinner party and there are some lighter, chilled soups for a perfect summer lunch.

Four chapters provide a wealth of recipes for all seasons and occasions. **Rich & Creamy Soups** offers much-loved classics, such as Cream of Mushroom Soup, as well as some innovative ideas based on cuisines from countries as far apart as Morocco and Bali, India and Italy. **Spicy Soups** will not only set the taste buds tingling, but also give the imaginative and adventurous cook a marvellous opportunity to experiment with some unusual ingredients, from groundnut (peanut) paste to pickled mustard leaves, and from okra to christophenes (chayotes). More familiar, but no less piquant

ingredients also feature in this chapter. Why not try Squash Soup with Horse-radish Cream or Curried Salmon Soup – both of them astonishingly quick and easy to prepare?

Chunky Soups offers dishes you can really get your teeth into. Many of them are packed to bursting with delicious fresh vegetables, whether the sweet-tasting early crops of spring and summer or filling and flavoursome potatoes, parsnips, carrots and turnips that provide inner fuel against the winter's chill.

Last, but very far from least, **One-pot-meal Soups** are the perfect solution to midweek suppers and family lunches

at busy weekends. They range from subtly flavoured Asian soups, served with a good helping of noodles, to gumbo, which is more like a fully-fledged stew.

Soups are versatile and adaptable, whatever your tastes – chicken, beef, fish, shellfish, vegetables or pasta can all play major or minor, separate or ensemble roles. Many can be made quickly with minimal effort, for maximum return. Serve them with fresh crusty bread or a slice of well-flavoured cheese and, at little expense or effort, you have a satisfying, nourishing and, above all, delicious meal.

Making Your Own Stocks

Fresh stocks are indispensable for creating good home-made soups. They add a depth of flavour that plain water just cannot achieve. Although many supermarkets now sell tubs of fresh stock, making your own is surprisingly easy, tastier and they're much more nutritious too.

Vegetable Stock

Use this versatile stock as the basis for all vegetarian soups.

INGREDIENTS

Makes 2.5 litres/4½ pints/11 cups

2 leeks, roughly chopped
3 celery sticks, roughly chopped
1 large onion, with skin, chopped
2 pieces fresh root ginger, chopped
1 yellow (bell) pepper, seeded
    and chopped
1 parsnip, chopped
mushroom stalks
tomato peelings
45ml/3 tbsp light soy sauce
3 bay leaves
a bunch of parsley stalks
3 sprigs of fresh thyme
1 sprig of fresh rosemary
10ml/2 tsp salt
freshly ground black pepper
3.5 litres/6 pints/15 cups cold water

1 Put all the ingredients into a very large pan. Bring slowly to the boil, then lower the heat and simmer for 30 minutes, stirring from time to time. Allow to cool.

2 Strain, then discard the vegetables. The stock is ready to use. Alternatively, chill or freeze it.

Meat Stock

The most delicious meat soups rely on a good home-made stock for success. Meat stock can be kept in the refrigerator for 4–5 days, or frozen for longer storage.

INGREDIENTS

Makes about 2 litres/3½ pints/9 cups

1.75kg/4lb beef bones, such as shin, leg,
    neck and shank, or veal or lamb bones,
    cut into 6cm/2½in pieces
2 onions, unpeeled, quartered
2 carrots, roughly chopped
2 celery sticks, with leaves if possible,
    roughly chopped
2 tomatoes, coarsely chopped
4.5 litres/7½ pints/20 cups cold water
a handful of parsley stalks
few sprigs of fresh thyme or 3.5ml/¾ tsp
    dried thyme
2 bay leaves
10 black peppercorns, lightly crushed

1 Preheat the oven to 230°C/450°F/Gas 8. Put the bones in a roasting tin (pan) and roast, for 30 minutes until they brown.

2 Add the onions, carrots, celery and tomatoes and baste with the fat in the tin. Roast for 20–30 minutes. Stir and baste occasionally.

3 Transfer the bones and roasted vegetables to a stockpot. Spoon off the fat from the roasting tin.

4 Add a little of the water to the roasting tin and bring to the boil on top of the stove, stirring well to scrape up any browned bits. Pour this liquid into the stockpot.

5 Add the remaining water to the pot. Bring just to the boil, skimming frequently to remove all the foam from the surface. Add the parsley, thyme, bay leaves and peppercorns.

6 Partly cover the stockpot and simmer the stock for 4–6 hours. The bones and vegetables should always be covered with liquid, so top up with a little boiling water from time to time if necessary.

7 Strain the stock through a colander or muslin, then skim as much fat as possible from the surface. If possible, cool the stock and then chill in the refrigerator; the fat will rise to the top and set in a layer that can be removed easily.

Chicken Stock

A good home-made poultry stock is invaluable in the kitchen. If poultry giblets are available, add them (except the livers) with the wings. Once made, chicken stock can be kept in an airtight container in the refrigerator for 3–4 days, or frozen for longer storage (up to 6 months).

INGREDIENTS

Makes about 2.5 litres/4 ½ pints/11 cups

1.2–1.5kg/2½–3lb chicken or turkey
   (wings, backs and necks)
2 onions, unpeeled, quartered
1 tbsp olive oil
4 litres/7 pints/17½ cups cold water
2 carrots, roughly chopped
2 celery sticks, with leaves if possible,
   roughly chopped
a small handful of fresh parsley
a few sprigs of fresh thyme or
   3.5ml/¾ tsp dried thyme
1 or 2 bay leaves
10 black peppercorns, lightly crushed

1 Combine the poultry wings, backs and necks in a stockpot with the onion quarters and the oil. Cook over moderate heat, stirring occasionally, until the poultry and onions are lightly and evenly browned.

2 Add the water and stir well to mix in the sediment on the bottom of the pan. Bring to the boil and skim off the impurities as they rise to the surface of the stock.

3 Add the chopped carrots and celery, fresh parsley, thyme, bay leaf and black peppercorns. Partly cover the stockpot and gently simmer the stock for about 3 hours.

4 Strain the stock through a sieve into a bowl and leave to cool, then chill in the refrigerator for an hour.

5 When cold, carefully remove the layer of fat that will have set on the surface. Store in the refrigerator for 3–4 days or freeze until required.

> ### COOK'S TIP
> ∽
> If you are making a large batch of stock, freeze it in small quantities in ice cube trays, but remember to label them for easy identification later.

Fish Stock

Fish stock is much quicker to make than poultry or meat stock. Ask your fishmonger for heads, bones and trimmings from white fish.

INGREDIENTS

Makes about 1 litre/ 1¾ pints/4 cups

675g/1½ lb heads, bones and trimmings
   from white fish
1 onion, sliced
2 celery sticks with leaves, chopped
1 carrot, sliced
½ lemon, sliced (optional)
1 bay leaf
a few sprigs of fresh parsley
6 black peppercorns
1.35 litres/2¼ pints/6 cups cold water
150ml/¼ pint/⅔ cup dry white wine

1 Rinse the fish heads, bones and trimmings well under cold running water. Put the bones in a stockpot with the vegetables and lemon, if using, the herbs, peppercorns, water and wine. Bring to the boil, skimming the surface frequently, then reduce the heat and simmer for 25 minutes.

2 Strain the stock without pressing down on the ingredients in the strainer. If not using immediately, leave to cool and then chill in the refrigerator. Fish stock should be stored in the refrigerator and used within 2 days, or it can be frozen for up to 3 months.

RICH &
CREAMY SOUPS

V

Broccoli and Almond Soup

The creaminess of the toasted almonds combines perfectly with the slightly bitter taste of the broccoli.

INGREDIENTS

Serves 4–6

50g/2oz/½ cup ground almonds

675g/1½ lb broccoli

900ml/1½ pints/3¾ cups vegetable stock
  or water

300ml/½ pint/1¼ cups skimmed milk

salt and freshly ground black pepper

1 Preheat the oven to 180°C/ 350°F/ Gas 4. Spread the ground almonds evenly on a baking sheet and toast in the oven for about 10 minutes until golden. Reserve one-quarter of the almonds and set aside to garnish the finished dish.

2 Cut the broccoli into small florets and steam for about 6–7 minutes until tender.

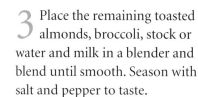

3 Place the remaining toasted almonds, broccoli, stock or water and milk in a blender and blend until smooth. Season with salt and pepper to taste.

4 Reheat the soup and serve sprinkled with the reserved toasted almonds.

Broccoli and Stilton Soup

*This is a really easy but rich soup –
choose something simple to follow,
such as plainly roasted or grilled
meat, poultry or fish.*

INGREDIENTS

Serves 4

350g/12oz broccoli

25g/1oz/2 tbsp butter

1 onion, chopped

1 leek, white part only, chopped

1 small potato, cut into chunks

600ml/1 pint/2½ cups hot chicken stock

300ml/½ pint/1¼ cups milk

45ml/3 tbsp double (heavy) cream

115g/4oz Stilton cheese, rind
  removed, crumbled

salt and freshly ground black pepper

1 Break the broccoli into florets,
discarding any tough stems.
Set aside two small florets to
garnish the finished dish.

2 Melt the butter in a large pan
and cook the onion and leek
until soft but not coloured. Add
the broccoli and potato, then pour
in the stock. Cover and simmer for
15–20 minutes, until the vegetables
are tender.

3 Cool slightly, then pour into a
blender or food processor and
purée until smooth. Strain the
mixture through a sieve back into
the rinsed pan.

4 Add the milk and cream to the
pan. Season to taste with salt
and freshly ground black pepper.
Reheat gently. At the last minute
add the cheese, stirring until it just
melts. Do not boil.

5 Meanwhile, blanch the
reserved broccoli florets and
cut them vertically into thin slices.
Ladle the soup into warmed bowls
and garnish with the sliced
broccoli and a generous grinding
of black pepper.

Tomato and Blue Cheese Soup

The concentrated flavour of roasted tomatoes strikes a great balance with strong blue cheese.

INGREDIENTS

Serves 4

1.5kg/3lb ripe tomatoes, peeled, quartered
   and seeded
2 garlic cloves, minced (ground)
30ml/2 tbsp vegetable oil or butter
1 leek, chopped
1 carrot, chopped
1.2 litres/2 pints/5 cups chicken stock
115g/4oz blue cheese, crumbled
45ml/3 tbsp whipping cream
several large fresh basil leaves, or 1–2 fresh
   parsley sprigs, plus extra to garnish
175g/6oz bacon, cooked and crumbled,
   to garnish
salt and freshly ground black pepper

1 Preheat the oven to 200°C/
400°F/Gas 6. Spread the
tomatoes in a shallow ovenproof
dish. Sprinkle with the garlic and
some salt and pepper. Place in the
oven and bake for 35 minutes.

2 Heat the oil or butter in a large
pan. Add the leek and carrot
and season lightly with salt and
pepper. Cook over low heat,
stirring often, for about 10 minutes
until softened.

3 Stir in the stock and baked
tomatoes. Bring to the boil,
then lower the heat, cover and
simmer for about 20 minutes.

4 Add the blue cheese, cream
and basil or parsley. Transfer
to a food processor or blender and
process until smooth (work in
batches if necessary). Taste and
adjust the seasoning.

5 Reheat the soup, but do not
boil. Serve garnished with
bacon and a sprig of fresh herbs.

Cauliflower and Walnut Cream

Even though there's no cream added to this soup, the cauliflower gives it a delicious, rich, creamy texture.

INGREDIENTS

Serves 4

1 medium cauliflower

1 medium onion, roughly chopped

450ml/¾ pint/scant 2 cups chicken or
    vegetable stock

450ml/¾ pint/scant 2 cups skimmed milk

45ml/3 tbsp walnut pieces

salt and freshly ground black pepper

paprika and chopped walnuts, to garnish

1 Trim the cauliflower of outer leaves and break into small florets. Place the cauliflower, onion and stock in a large pan.

2 Bring to the boil, cover and simmer for about 15 minutes until soft. Add the milk and walnut pieces, then purée in a blender or food processor until smooth.

3 Season the soup to taste with salt and pepper, then reheat and bring to the boil. Serve sprinkled with a dusting of paprika and chopped walnuts.

VARIATION

If you prefer, you can make this soup using broccoli instead of cauliflower.

Carrot and Coriander Soup

Use a good home-made stock for this soup – it adds depth of flavour.

INGREDIENTS

Serves 4

50g/2oz/4 tbsp butter

3 leeks, sliced

450g/1lb carrots, sliced

15ml/1 tbsp ground coriander

1.2 litres/2 pints/5 cups chicken stock

150ml/¼ pint/⅔ cup Greek-style
   (US strained plain) yogurt

salt and freshly ground black pepper

30–45ml/2–3 tbsp chopped fresh
   coriander (cilantro), to garnish

1 Melt the butter in a large pan. Add the leeks and carrots and stir well. Cover and cook for 10 minutes, until the vegetables are beginning to soften.

2 Stir in the ground coriander and cook for about 1 minute. Pour in the stock and add seasoning to taste. Bring to the boil, cover and simmer for about 20 minutes, until the leeks and carrots are tender.

3 Leave to cool slightly, then purée the soup in a blender until smooth. Return the soup to the pan and add 30ml/2 tbsp of the yogurt, then taste the soup and adjust the seasoning. Reheat gently, but do not boil.

4 Ladle the soup into bowls and put a spoonful of the remaining yogurt in the centre of each. Scatter over the chopped coriander and serve immediately.

Green Bean and Parmesan Soup

Fresh green beans and Parmesan cheese make a simple but delicious combination of flavours.

INGREDIENTS

Serves 4

25g/1oz/2 tbsp butter or margarine

225g/8oz green beans, trimmed

1 garlic clove, crushed

450ml/³⁄₄ pint/scant 2 cups vegetable stock

40g/1¹⁄₂ oz/¹⁄₂ cup grated Parmesan cheese

50ml/2fl oz/¹⁄₄ cup single (light) cream

salt and freshly ground black pepper

30ml/2 tbsp chopped fresh parsley, to garnish

1 Melt the butter or margarine in a medium pan. Add the green beans and garlic and cook for 2–3 minutes over a medium heat, stirring frequently.

2 Stir in the stock and season with salt and pepper. Bring to the boil, then simmer, uncovered, for 10–15 minutes until the beans are tender.

3 Pour the soup into a blender or food processor and process until smooth. Alternatively, purée the soup in a food mill. Return to the pan and reheat gently.

4 Stir in the Parmesan and cream. Sprinkle with the parsley and serve.

Moroccan Vegetable Soup

Creamy parsnip and pumpkin give this soup a wonderfully rich texture.

INGREDIENTS

Serves 4

15ml/1 tbsp olive or sunflower oil

15g/½ oz/1 tbsp butter

1 onion, chopped

225g/8oz carrots, chopped

225g/8oz parsnips, chopped

225g/8oz pumpkin

about 900ml/1½ pints/3¾ cups vegetable
    or chicken stock

lemon juice, to taste

salt and freshly ground black pepper

For the garnish

7.5ml/1½ tsp olive oil

½ garlic clove, finely chopped

45ml/3 tbsp chopped fresh parsley and
    coriander (cilantro), mixed

a good pinch of paprika

1 Heat the oil and butter in a large pan and fry the onion for about 3 minutes until softened, stirring occasionally. Add the carrots and parsnips, stir well, cover and cook over a gentle heat for a further 5 minutes.

2 Cut the pumpkin into chunks, discarding the skin and pith, and stir into the pan. Cover and cook for a further 5 minutes, then add the stock and seasoning and slowly bring to the boil. Cover and simmer for 35–40 minutes until the vegetables are tender.

3 Leave the soup to cool slightly, then pour in to a food processor or blender and purée until smooth, adding a little extra water if the soup seems too thick. Pour back into a clean pan and reheat gently.

4 To make the garnish, heat the oil in a small pan and fry the garlic and herbs for 2 minutes. Add the paprika and stir well.

5 Adjust the seasoning of the soup and stir in lemon juice to taste. Pour into bowls and spoon a little of the prepared garnish on top, which should then be swirled carefully into the soup.

Creamy Courgette and Dolcelatte Soup

V

The beauty of this soup is its delicate colour, its creamy texture and its subtle taste.

INGREDIENTS

Serves 4–6

30ml/2 tbsp olive oil

15g/½ oz/1 tbsp butter

1 medium onion, roughly chopped

900g/2lb courgettes (zucchini), trimmed and sliced

5ml/1 tsp dried oregano

about 600ml/1 pint/2½ cups vegetable stock

115g/4oz Dolcelatte cheese, rind removed, diced

300ml/½ pint/1¼ cups single (light) cream

salt and freshly ground black pepper

To garnish

sprigs of fresh oregano

extra Dolcelatte cheese

1 Heat the oil and butter in a large pan until foaming. Add the onion and cook gently for about 5 minutes, stirring frequently, until softened but not brown.

2 Add the courgettes and oregano, with salt and pepper to taste. Cook over a medium heat for 10 minutes, stirring frequently.

3 Pour in the stock and bring to the boil, stirring frequently. Lower the heat, half-cover the pan and simmer gently, stirring occasionally, for about 30 minutes. Stir in the diced Dolcelatte until it is melted.

4 Process the soup in a blender or food processor until smooth, then press through a sieve into a clean pan.

5 Add two-thirds of the cream and stir over a low heat until hot, but not boiling. Check the consistency and add more stock if the soup is too thick. Taste and adjust the seasoning if necessary.

6 Pour into heated bowls. Swirl in the remaining cream, garnish with fresh oregano and extra Dolcelatte cheese, crumbled, and serve.

Fresh Pea Soup St Germain

This soup takes its name from a suburb of Paris where peas used to be cultivated in market gardens.

INGREDIENTS

Serves 2–3

a small knob (pat) of butter

2 or 3 shallots, finely chopped

400g/14oz/3 cups shelled fresh peas (from about 1.5kg/3lb garden peas)

500ml/17fl oz/2¼ cups water

45–60ml/3–4 tbsp whipping cream (optional)

salt and freshly ground black pepper

croûtons, to garnish

3 When the peas are tender, ladle them into a food processor or blender with a little of the cooking liquid and process until smooth.

4 Strain the soup into the pan or casserole, stir in the whipping cream, if using, and heat through without boiling. Add seasoning to taste and serve hot, garnished with croûtons.

COOK'S TIP

If fresh peas are not available, use frozen peas, but thaw and rinse them before use.

1 Melt the butter in a heavy pan or flameproof casserole. Add the chopped shallots and cook for about 3 minutes, stirring them occasionally.

2 Add the peas and water and season with salt and a little pepper. Cover and simmer for about 12 minutes for young peas and up to 18 minutes for large or older peas, stirring occasionally.

Watercress Soup

V

A delicious and nutritious soup which should be served with crusty bread.

INGREDIENTS

Serves 4

15ml/1 tbsp sunflower oil

15g/¹⁄₂ oz/1 tbsp butter

1 medium onion, finely chopped

1 medium potato, diced

about 175g/6oz watercress

400ml/14fl oz/1²⁄₃ cups vegetable stock

400ml/14fl oz/1²⁄₃ cups milk

lemon juice, to taste

salt and freshly ground black pepper

sour cream, to serve

1 Heat the oil and butter in a large pan and cook the onion over a gentle heat until soft but not browned. Add the potato, cook gently for 2–3 minutes and then cover and sweat for 5 minutes over a gentle heat, stirring from time to time.

2 Strip the watercress leaves from the stalks and roughly chop the stalks.

COOK'S TIP

Provided you leave out the sour cream, this is a low-calorie soup.

3 Add the stock and milk to the pan, stir in the chopped stalks and season. Bring to the boil and simmer gently, partially covered, for 10–12 minutes until the potatoes are tender. Add all but a few of the watercress leaves and simmer for 2 minutes more.

4 Process the soup in a food processor or blender and then pour into a clean pan and heat gently with the reserved watercress leaves.

5 Taste the soup when hot, add a little lemon juice and adjust the seasoning.

6 Pour the soup into warmed soup bowls and garnish with a little sour cream in the centre just before serving.

Cream of Spinach Soup

V

*This is a deliciously creamy soup
that you will want to make often.*

Serves 4

25g/1oz/2 tbsp butter

1 small onion, chopped

675g/1½lb fresh spinach, chopped

1.2 litres/2 pints/5 cups vegetable stock

50g/2oz creamed coconut (coconut cream)

freshly grated nutmeg

300ml/½ pint/1¼ cups single
   (light) cream

salt and freshly ground black pepper

chopped fresh chives, to garnish

3 Return the mixture to the pan
  and add the remaining stock
and the creamed coconut, with
salt, pepper and nutmeg to taste.
Simmer for 15 minutes to thicken.

4 Add the cream to the pan,
  stir well and heat through, but
do not boil. Serve hot, garnished
with long strips of chives.

1 Melt the butter in a pan over
  a moderate heat and sauté the
onion for a few minutes until
soft. Add the spinach, cover the
pan and cook gently for 10
minutes, until the spinach has
wilted and reduced.

2 Pour the spinach mixture into
  a blender or food processor
and add a little of the stock. Blend
until smooth.

Cream of Red Pepper Soup

Grilling peppers gives them a sweet, smoky flavour which is quite unlike their raw or steamed flavour. They are delicious in this velvety soup which has a hint of rosemary to add aromatic depth.

INGREDIENTS

Serves 4

4 red (bell) peppers

25g/1oz/2 tbsp butter

1 onion, finely chopped

1 sprig of fresh rosemary

1.2 litres/2 pints/5 cups chicken or light
   vegetable stock

45ml/3 tbsp tomato purée (paste)

120ml/4fl oz/$^1\!/_2$ cup double (heavy) cream

paprika

salt and freshly ground black pepper

1 Preheat the grill (broiler). Put the peppers in the grill pan under the grill and turn them regularly until the skins have blackened all round. Put them into plastic bags, sealing them closed. Leave them for 20 minutes.

2 Peel the blackened skin off the peppers. If possible avoid rinsing them under running water as this loses some of the natural oil and hence the flavour.

3 Halve the peppers, removing the seeds, stalks and pith, then roughly chop the flesh.

4 Melt the butter in a deep pan. Add the onion and rosemary and cook gently over a low heat for about 5 minutes. Remove the rosemary and discard.

5 Add the peppers and stock to the onion, bring to the boil and simmer for 15 minutes. Stir in the tomato purée, then process or sieve the soup to a smooth purée.

6 Stir in half the cream and season with paprika, salt, if necessary, and pepper.

7 Serve the soup hot or chilled, with the remaining cream swirled delicately on top. Speckle the cream very lightly with a pinch of paprika.

Cream of Avocado Soup

Avocados make wonderful soup –
pretty, delicious and refreshing.

INGREDIENTS

Serves 4

2 large ripe avocados

1 litre/1¾ pints/4 cups chicken stock

250ml/8fl oz/1 cup single (light) cream

salt and freshly ground white pepper

15ml/1 tbsp finely chopped fresh
    coriander (cilantro), to
    garnish (optional)

1 Cut the avocados in half, remove the stones (pits) and mash the flesh. Put the flesh into a sieve and press it through the sieve with a wooden spoon into a warm soup bowl.

2 Heat the chicken stock with the cream in a pan. When the mixture is hot, but not boiling, whisk it into the puréed avocado in the bowl.

3 Season to taste with salt and pepper. Serve immediately, sprinkled with the coriander, if using. The soup may be served chilled, if preferred.

Cream of Spring Onion Soup

V

The oniony flavour of this soup is surprisingly delicate.

INGREDIENTS

Serves 4–6

25g/1oz/2 tbsp butter

1 small onion, chopped

150g/5oz/1¾ cups spring onions (scallions)

225g/8oz potatoes, peeled and chopped

600ml/1 pint/2½ cups vegetable stock

350ml/12fl oz/1½ cups single
   (light) cream

30ml/2 tbsp lemon juice

salt and freshly ground white pepper

chopped fresh chives, to garnish

1 Melt the butter in a pan and add all the onions. Cover and cook over very low heat for about 10 minutes or until soft.

2 Add the potatoes and the stock. Bring to the boil, then cover again and simmer over moderately low heat for about 30 minutes. Cool slightly.

3 Purée the soup in a blender or food processor.

4 If serving the soup hot, pour it back into the pan. Add the cream and season with salt and pepper. Reheat gently, stirring occasionally. Add the lemon juice.

5 If serving the soup cold, pour it into a bowl. Stir in the cream and lemon juice and season with salt and freshly ground white pepper. Cover the bowl and chill for at least 1 hour.

6 Sprinkle with the chopped chives before serving.

V

Fresh Mushroom Soup with Tarragon

This is a light mushroom soup, subtly flavoured with tarragon.

INGREDIENTS

Serves 6

15g/½ oz/1 tbsp butter or margarine

4 shallots, finely chopped

450g/11b/6 cups chestnut mushrooms, finely chopped

300ml/½ pint/1¼ cups vegetable stock

300ml/½ pint/ 1¼ cups semi-skimmed (low-fat) milk

15–30ml/1–2 tbsp chopped fresh tarragon

30ml/2 tbsp dry sherry (optional)

salt and freshly ground black pepper

sprigs of fresh tarragon, to garnish

1 Melt the butter or margarine in a large pan, add the shallots and cook gently for 5 minutes, stirring occasionally. Add the mushrooms and cook gently for 3 minutes, stirring. Add the stock and milk.

2 Bring to the boil, then cover and simmer gently for about 20 minutes until the vegetables are soft. Stir in the chopped tarragon and season to taste with salt and pepper.

3 Leave the soup to cool slightly, then purée in a blender or food processor, in batches if necessary, until smooth. Return the soup to the rinsed-out pan and reheat gently.

4 Stir in the sherry, if using, then ladle the soup into warmed soup bowls and serve garnished with sprigs of tarragon.

VARIATION

If you prefer, use a mixture of wild and button (white) mushrooms instead.

Balinese Vegetable Soup

V

Any seasonal vegetables can be used in this soup, which is known as Sayur Oelih.

INGREDIENTS

Serves 8

225g/8oz green beans

1.2 litres/2 pints/5 cups boiling water

400ml/14fl oz/1²⁄₃ cups coconut milk

1 garlic clove

2 macadamia nuts or 4 almonds

1cm/¹⁄₂ in cube shrimp paste

10–15ml/2–3 tsp coriander seeds, dry-fried and ground

oil, for frying

1 onion, finely sliced

2 duan salam or bay leaves

225g/8oz beansprouts

30ml/2 tbsp lemon juice

salt

1 Trim the green beans and cut them into small pieces. Cook the beans in the boiling water, salted, for 3–4 minutes. Drain the beans and reserve the cooking water.

2 Spoon off 45–60ml/3–4 tbsp of the cream from the top of the coconut milk and set aside.

3 Grind the garlic, nuts, shrimp paste and ground coriander to a paste in a food processor or with a pestle and mortar.

4 Heat the oil in a pan and fry the onion until transparent. Remove from the pan and reserve. Fry the paste for 2 minutes without browning. Pour in the reserved bean cooking water and coconut milk. Bring to the boil and add the duan salam or bay leaves. Cook, uncovered, for 15–20 minutes.

5 Just before serving, add the beans, fried onion, beansprouts, reserved coconut cream and lemon juice. Taste and adjust the seasoning, if necessary. Serve immediately.

Cream of Celeriac and Spinach Soup

V

Celeriac has a wonderful flavour that is reminiscent of celery, but also adds a slightly nutty taste. Here it is combined with spinach to make a delicious soup.

INGREDIENTS

Serves 6

1 litre/1¾ pints/4 cups water

250ml/8fl oz/1 cup dry white wine

1 leek, thickly sliced

500g/1¼ lb celeriac, diced

200g/7oz fresh spinach leaves

freshly grated nutmeg

salt and freshly ground black pepper

25g/1oz/¼ cup pine nuts, to garnish

1 Mix the water and wine in a jug (pitcher). Place the leek, celeriac and spinach in a deep pan and pour the liquid over the top. Bring to the boil, lower the heat and simmer for 10–15 minutes until the vegetables are soft.

2 Pour the celeriac mixture into a blender or food processor and purée until smooth, in batches if necessary. Return to the clean pan and season to taste with salt, ground black pepper and nutmeg. Reheat gently.

3 Heat a non-stick frying pan (do not add any oil) and add the pine nuts. Roast until golden brown, stirring occasionally so that they do not stick. Sprinkle them over the soup and serve.

COOK'S TIP

If the soup is too thick, thin with a little water or semi-skimmed (low-fat) milk when puréeing.

Creamy Tomato Soup

Tomato soup is an old favourite. This version is made special by the addition of fresh herbs and cream.

INGREDIENTS

Serves 4

25g/1oz/2 tbsp butter or margarine

1 onion, chopped

900g/2lb tomatoes, peeled and quartered

2 carrots, chopped

450ml/¾ pint/scant 2 cups chicken stock

30ml/2 tbsp chopped fresh parsley

2.5ml/½ tsp fresh thyme leaves, plus extra
   to garnish

75ml/5 tbsp whipping cream

salt and freshly ground black pepper

1 Melt the butter or margarine in a large pan. Add the onion and cook, stirring occasionally, for 5 minutes until softened.

2 Stir in the tomatoes, carrots, chicken stock, parsley and thyme. Bring to the boil. Reduce the heat to low, cover the pan, and simmer for 15–20 minutes until the vegetables are tender.

3 Purée the soup in a vegetable mill until it is smooth. Return the puréed soup to the pan.

4 Stir in the cream, and reheat gently without boiling. Season the soup to taste with salt and freshly ground black pepper. Ladle into warmed soup bowls and serve piping hot, garnished with fresh thyme leaves.

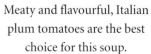

COOK'S TIP

Meaty and flavourful, Italian plum tomatoes are the best choice for this soup.

Cream of Mushroom Soup

V

A good mushroom soup makes the most of the subtle and sometimes rather elusive flavour of mushrooms. Button mushrooms are used here for their pale colour; chestnut or, better still, field mushrooms give a fuller flavour.

INGREDIENTS

Serves 4

275g/10oz button (white) mushrooms

15ml/1 tbsp sunflower oil

40g/1½ oz/3 tbsp butter

1 small onion, finely chopped

15ml/1 tbsp plain (all-purpose) flour

450ml/¾ pint/scant 2 cups vegetable stock

450ml/¾ pint/scant 2 cups milk

a pinch of dried basil

30–45ml/2–3 tbsp single (light) cream

salt and freshly ground black pepper

fresh basil leaves, to garnish

1 Separate the mushroom caps from the stalks. Finely slice the caps and finely chop the stalks.

2 Heat the oil and half the butter in a heavy pan and add the onion, mushroom stalks and about three-quarters of the sliced mushroom caps. Fry for about 1–2 minutes, stirring frequently, then cover and sweat over a gentle heat for 6–7 minutes, stirring from time to time.

3 Stir in the flour and cook for about 1 minute. Gradually add the stock and milk, to make a smooth, thin sauce. Add the dried basil, and season to taste. Bring to the boil and simmer, partly covered, for 15 minutes.

4 Cool the soup slightly and then pour into a food processor or blender and process until smooth. Melt the rest of the butter in a frying pan and fry the remaining mushroom caps gently for 3 minutes until they are just tender.

5 Pour the soup into a clean pan and stir in the fried mushrooms. Heat until very hot and adjust the seasoning. Add the cream. Serve sprinkled with fresh basil leaves.

Egg and Cheese Soup

In this classic Roman soup, eggs and cheese are beaten into hot broth, producing a slightly "curdled" texture, which is a characteristic of the dish.

INGREDIENTS

Serves 6

3 eggs

45ml/3 tbsp fine semolina

90ml/6 tbsp grated Parmesan cheese

a pinch of freshly grated nutmeg

1.5 litres/2½ pints/6¼ cups meat or
   chicken stock

salt and freshly ground black pepper

12 slices French bread, to serve

1 Beat the eggs in a bowl with the semolina and cheese. Add the nutmeg. Beat in 250ml/8fl oz/ 1 cup of the cool stock.

2 Meanwhile, heat the leftover stock to simmering point in a large pan.

3 When the stock is hot, whisk the egg mixture into the stock. Raise the heat slightly and bring it barely to the boil. Season with salt and pepper. Cook for 4 minutes. As the egg cooks, the soup will lose its smooth consistency.

4 To serve, toast the slices of French bread and place two of them in the bottom of each soup plate. Ladle the hot soup on top of the bread and serve immediately.

Creamy Sweetcorn Soup

This is simple to prepare yet full of flavour. It is sometimes made with sour cream and cream cheese. Poblano chillies may be added, but these are rather difficult to locate outside Mexico.

INGREDIENTS

Serves 4

30ml/2 tbsp corn oil

1 onion, finely chopped

1 red (bell) pepper, seeded and chopped

450g/1lb/2²/₃ cups sweetcorn kernels, thawed if frozen

750ml/1¼ pints/3 cups chicken stock

250ml/8fl oz/1 cup single (light)cream

salt and freshly ground black pepper

½ red (bell) pepper, seeded and finely diced, to garnish

3 Transfer the mixture to a heavy pan and stir in the stock. Season to taste with salt and pepper, bring to a simmer and cook for 5 minutes.

4 Gently stir in the cream. Serve the soup hot or chilled, sprinkled with the diced red pepper. If serving hot, reheat gently after adding the cream, but do not allow the soup to boil.

1 Heat the oil in a frying pan and sauté the onion and chopped red pepper for about 5 minutes, until soft. Add the sweetcorn and sauté for 2 minutes.

2 Carefully tip the contents of the pan into a food processor or blender. Process until smooth, scraping down the sides of the blender and adding a little of the stock, if necessary.

White Bean Soup

Use haricot beans or butter beans for this velvety soup.

INGREDIENTS

Serves 4

175g/6oz/¾ cup dried haricot (navy) or
   butter (lima) beans, soaked overnight
30–45ml/2–3 tbsp oil
2 large onions, chopped
4 celery sticks, chopped
1 parsnip, chopped
1 litre/1¾ pints/4 cups chicken stock
salt and freshly ground black pepper
chopped fresh coriander (cilantro) and
   paprika, to garnish

1 Drain the beans and boil rapidly in fresh water for 10 minutes. Drain, cover with more fresh water and simmer for 1–2 hours until soft. Reserve the liquid and discard any bean skins on the surface.

2 Heat the oil in a heavy pan and sauté the onions, celery and parsnip for 3 minutes.

3 Add the cooked beans and stock and continue cooking until the vegetables are tender. Leave the soup to cool slightly and, using a food processor or hand blender, blend the soup until it is velvety smooth.

4 Reheat the soup gently, gradually adding some of the bean liquid or a little water if it is too thick. Season to taste.

5 To serve, transfer the soup into wide bowls. Garnish with fresh coriander and paprika.

COOK'S TIP

You can, if you prefer, use a 400g/14oz can cannellini or butter (lima) beans instead of dried beans. Drain and rinse them before adding to the dish.

Prawn Bisque

The classic French method for making a bisque requires pushing the shellfish through a tamis, or drum sieve. This recipe is simpler and the result is just as smooth.

INGREDIENTS

Serves 6-8

675g/1½lb small or medium cooked
    prawns (shrimp) in their shells
25ml/1½ tbsp vegetable oil
2 onions, halved and sliced
1 large carrot, sliced
2 celery sticks, sliced
2 litres/3½ pints/9 cups water
a few drops of lemon juice
30ml/2 tbsp tomato purée (paste)
bouquet garni
50g/2oz/4 tbsp butter
50g/2oz/⅓ cup plain (all-purpose) flour
45–60ml/3–4 tbsp brandy
150ml/¼ pint/⅔ cup whipping cream

1 Remove the heads from the prawns and peel away the shells. Reserve the heads and shells for the stock. Place the prawns in a covered bowl in the refrigerator.

2 Heat the oil in a large pan, add the heads and shells and cook over a high heat, stirring, until they start to brown. Reduce the heat to medium, add the vegetables and cook, stirring occasionally, for 5 minutes until the onions soften.

3 Add the water, lemon juice, tomato purée and bouquet garni. Bring the stock to the boil, then reduce the heat, cover and simmer gently for 25 minutes. Strain the stock through a sieve.

4 Melt the butter in a heavy pan over a medium heat. Stir in the flour and cook until just golden, stirring occasionally.

5 Add the brandy. Gradually pour in half the prawn stock, whisking vigorously until smooth, then whisk in the remaining liquid. Season if necessary. Reduce the heat, cover and simmer for 5 minutes, stirring frequently.

6 Strain the soup into a clean pan. Add the cream and a little extra lemon juice to taste, then stir in most of the reserved prawns and cook over a medium heat, stirring frequently, until hot. Serve at once, garnished with the remaining reserved prawns.

COOK'S TIP

If you prefer you may leave the brandy out of this dish and it will still taste delicious.

Shrimp and Corn Bisque

Hot pepper sauce brings a touch of spice to this mild, creamy soup.

Serves 4

30ml/2 tbsp olive oil

1 onion, finely minced (ground)

50g/2oz/4 tbsp butter

25g/1oz/¼ cup plain (all-purpose) flour

750ml/1¼ pints/3 cups fish stock

250ml/8fl oz/1 cup milk

115g/4oz/1 cup peeled cooked small
    shrimp, deveined if necessary

225g/8oz/1½ cups sweetcorn kernels

2.5ml/½ tsp chopped fresh dill or thyme

hot pepper sauce

120ml/4fl oz/½ cup single (light) cream

salt

sprigs of fresh dill, to garnish

1 Heat the olive oil in a large heavy pan. Add the onion and cook over a low heat for 8–10 minutes until softened.

2 Meanwhile, melt the butter in a medium-size pan. Add the flour and cook for 1–2 minutes, stirring constantly. Stir in the stock and milk, bring to the boil and cook for 5–8 minutes, stirring frequently.

3 Cut each shrimp into two or three pieces and add to the onion with the corn and dill or thyme. Cook for 2 minutes, then remove from the heat.

4 Add the sauce mixture to the shrimp and corn mixture, and mix well. Remove 750ml/1¼ pints/ 3 cups of the soup and purée in a blender or food processor. Return it to the rest of the soup in the pan and stir well. Season with salt and hot pepper sauce to taste.

5 Add the cream and stir to blend. Heat the soup almost to boiling point, stirring frequently.

6 Divide among individual soup bowls and serve hot, garnished with sprigs of dill.

Fish and Sweet Potato Soup

The subtle sweetness of the potato, combined with the fish and the aromatic flavour of oregano, makes this an appetizing soup.

INGREDIENTS

Serves 4

$\frac{1}{2}$ onion, chopped

175g/6oz sweet potato, peeled and diced

175g/6oz boneless white fish
  fillet, skinned

50g/2oz carrot, chopped

5ml/1 tsp chopped fresh oregano or
  2.5ml/$\frac{1}{2}$ tsp dried oregano

2.5ml/$\frac{1}{2}$ tsp ground cinnamon

1.5 litres/2$\frac{1}{2}$ pints/6$\frac{1}{4}$ cups fish stock

75ml/5 tbsp single (light) cream

chopped fresh parsley, to garnish

1 Put the chopped onion, diced sweet potato, white fish, chopped carrot, oregano, cinnamon and half of the fish stock in a pan. Bring to the boil, then simmer for 20 minutes or until the potato is cooked.

2 Leave to cool, then pour into a blender or food processor and blend until smooth.

3 Return the soup to the pan, add the remaining fish stock and gently bring to the boil. Reduce the heat to low and add the cream, then gently heat without boiling, stirring occasionally.

4 Serve hot in warmed soup bowls, garnished with the chopped fresh parsley.

VARIATION

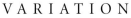

Garnish with chopped fresh tarragon instead of parsley.

Creamy Fish Chowder

A traditional soup that never fails to please, whether it is made with milk or more luxuriously, with a generous quantity of cream.

INGREDIENTS

Serves 4

3 thick-cut bacon rashers (strips)

1 large onion

675g/1½ lb potatoes

1 litre/1¾ pints/4 cups fish stock

450g/1lb skinless haddock, fillets cut into
   2.5cm/1in cubes

30ml/2 tbsp chopped fresh parsley

15ml/1 tbsp chopped fresh chives

300ml/½ pint/1¼ cups whipping cream
   or full-fat (whole) milk

salt and freshly ground black pepper

1 Remove the rind from the bacon and discard it; then cut the bacon into small pieces. Chop the onion and cut the potatoes into 2cm/¾in cubes.

2 Fry the bacon in a deep pan until the fat is rendered. Add the onion and potatoes and cook over low heat, without browning, for about 10 minutes. Season to taste with salt and pepper.

3 Pour off excess bacon fat from the pan. Add the fish stock to the pan and bring to a boil. Simmer for about 15–20 minutes, until the vegetables are tender.

4 Stir in the cubes of fish, the parsley and chives. Simmer for about 3–4 minutes, until the fish is just cooked.

5 Stir the cream or milk into the chowder and reheat gently, but do not bring to the boil. Season to taste with salt and pepper and serve immediately.

VARIATION

Cod fillets would be equally good in this chowder, or try smoked fillets for a stronger taste.

SPICY SOUPS

V

Yogurt Soup

Some communities in India add sugar to this soup.

INGREDIENTS

Serves 4–6

450ml/¾ pint/scant 2 cups natural (US plain) yogurt, beaten

25g/1oz/¼ cup gram flour (besan)

2.5ml/½ tsp chilli powder

2.5ml/½ tsp turmeric salt, to taste

2–3 fresh green chillies, finely chopped

60ml/4 tbsp vegetable oil

1 whole dried red chilli

5ml/1 tsp cumin seeds

3–4 curry leaves

3 garlic cloves, crushed

5cm/2in piece fresh root ginger, peeled

30ml/2 tbsp chopped fresh coriander (cilantro)

1 Mix together the yogurt, flour, chilli powder and turmeric salt and pass through a strainer into a pan. Add the green chillies and cook gently for about 10 minutes, stirring occasionally. Be careful not to let the soup boil over.

2 Heat the oil in a frying pan and fry the remaining spices with the garlic. Crush the ginger and add it to the pan, cook until the dried chilli turns black. Stir in 15ml/1 tbsp of the chopped fresh coriander.

3 Pour the spices over the yogurt soup, cover the pan and leave to rest for 5 minutes. Mix well and gently reheat for 5 minutes more. Serve hot, garnished with the remaining chopped coriander.

Spiced Parsnip Soup

This pale, creamy-textured soup is given a special touch with an aromatic, spiced garlic and coriander garnish.

Serves 4–6

40g/1¹⁄₂ oz/3 tbsp butter
1 onion, chopped
675g/1¹⁄₂ lb parsnips, diced
5ml/1 tsp ground coriander
2.5ml/¹⁄₂ tsp ground cumin
2.5ml/¹⁄₂ tsp ground turmeric
1.5ml/¹⁄₄ tsp chilli powder
1.2 litres/2 pints/5 cups chicken stock
150ml/¹⁄₄ pint/²⁄₃ cup single (light) cream
15ml/1 tbsp sunflower oil
1 garlic clove, cut into julienne strips
10ml/2 tsp yellow mustard seeds
salt and freshly ground black pepper

1 Melt the butter in a large pan, add the onion and parsnips and fry gently for about 3 minutes.

2 Stir in the spices and cook for 1 minute more. Add the stock, season with salt and pepper and bring to the boil.

3 Reduce the heat, cover and simmer for about 45 minutes, until the parsnips are tender. Cool slightly, then purée in a blender or food processor until smooth. Return the soup to the pan, add the cream and heat through gently over a low heat.

4 Heat the oil in a small pan, add the julienne strips of garlic and the yellow mustard seeds and fry quickly until the garlic begins to brown and the mustard seeds start to pop and splutter. Remove from the heat.

5 Ladle the soup into warmed soup bowls and pour a little of the hot spice mixture over each one. Serve immediately.

Pumpkin and Coconut Soup

Rich and sweet flavours are married beautifully with sharp and hot in this creamy South-east Asian-influenced soup.

INGREDIENTS

Serves 4–6

2 garlic cloves, crushed

4 shallots, finely crushed

2.5ml/$\frac{1}{2}$ tsp shrimp paste

15ml/1 tbsp dried shrimps, soaked
      for 10 minutes and drained

1 lemon grass stalk, chopped

2 fresh green chillies, seeded

600ml/1 pint/2$\frac{1}{2}$ cups chicken stock

450g/1lb pumpkin, cut into 2cm/$\frac{3}{4}$ in
      thick chunks

600ml/1 pint/2$\frac{1}{2}$ cups coconut cream

30ml/2 tbsp fish sauce (*nam pla*)

5ml/1 tsp sugar

115g/4oz small cooked peeled prawns
      (shrimp)

salt and freshly ground black pepper

2 fresh red chillies, seeded and finely
        sliced, to garnish

10–12 fresh basil leaves, to garnish

1 Using a pestle and mortar, grind the garlic, shallots, shrimp paste, dried shrimps, lemon grass, green chillies and a pinch of salt into a paste.

2 In a large pan, bring the chicken stock to the boil, add the paste and stir until dissolved.

3 Lower the heat, add the pumpkin, and simmer for about 10–15 minutes or until the pumpkin is tender.

4 Stir in the coconut cream, then bring back to a simmer. Add the fish sauce, sugar and ground black pepper to taste.

5 Add the prawns and cook until they are heated through. Serve garnished with the sliced red chillies and basil leaves.

COOK'S TIP
❧

Shrimp paste, which is made from ground shrimps fermented in brine, is used to give food a savoury flavour.

Green Lentil Soup

Lentil soup is an eastern Mediterranean classic, varying in its spiciness according to region. Red or puy lentils make an equally good substitute for the green lentils used in this version.

INGREDIENTS

Serves 4-6

225g/8oz/1 cup green lentils

75ml/5 tbsp olive oil

3 onions, finely chopped

2 garlic cloves, finely sliced

10ml/2 tsp cumin seeds, crushed

1.5ml/¼ tsp ground turmeric

600ml/1 pint/2½ cups vegetable stock

600ml/1 pint/2½ cups water

salt and freshly ground black pepper

30ml/2 tbsp roughly chopped fresh coriander (cilantro), to garnish

warm crusty bread, to serve

1 Put the lentils in a pan and cover with cold water. Bring to the boil and boil rapidly for 10 minutes. Drain.

2 Heat 30ml/2 tbsp of the oil in a pan and fry two of the onions with the garlic, cumin and turmeric for 3 minutes, stirring. Add the lentils, stock and water. Bring to the boil, reduce the heat, cover and simmer for 30 minutes until the lentils are soft.

3 Heat the remaining oil and fry the third onion until golden brown, stirring frequently.

4 Use a potato masher to lightly mash the lentils and make the soup pulpy in texture. Reheat gently and season with salt and freshly ground pepper to taste.

5 Pour the soup into bowls. Stir the fresh coriander in with the fried onion and scatter over the soup as a garnish. Serve with warm crusty bread.

COOK'S TIP

The lentils do not need to be soaked before cooking.

Squash Soup with Horseradish Cream

The combination of cream, curry powder and horseradish makes a wonderful topping for this beautiful golden soup.

INGREDIENTS

Serves 6

1 butternut squash

1 cooking apple

25g/1oz/2 tbsp butter

1 onion, finely chopped

5–10ml/1–2 tsp curry powder, plus extra to garnish

900ml/1½ pints/3¾ cups vegetable stock

5ml/1 tsp chopped fresh sage

150ml/¼ pint/⅔ cup apple juice

salt and freshly ground black pepper

lime shreds, to garnish (optional)

For the horseradish cream

60ml/4 tbsp double (heavy) cream

10ml/2 tsp horseradish sauce

2.5ml/½ tsp curry powder

1 Peel the squash, remove the seeds and chop the flesh. Peel, core and chop the apple.

2 Heat the butter in a large pan. Add the onion and cook, stirring occasionally, for 5 minutes until soft. Stir in the curry powder. Cook to bring out the flavour, stirring constantly, for 2 minutes.

3 Add the stock, squash, apple and sage. Bring to the boil, lower the heat, cover and simmer for 20 minutes until the squash and apple are soft.

4 Meanwhile, make the horseradish cream. Whip the cream in a bowl until stiff, then stir in the horseradish sauce and curry powder. Cover and chill until required.

5 Purée the soup in a blender or food processor. Return to the clean pan and add the apple juice, with salt and pepper to taste. Reheat gently, without boiling.

6 Serve the soup in bowls, topped with a spoonful of horseradish cream and a dusting of curry powder. Garnish with a few lime shreds, if you like.

Vegetable Soup with Coconut

The coconut gives a delicious flavour to this fine vegetable soup.

INGREDIENTS

Serves 4

25g/1 oz/2 tbsp butter or margarine

½ red onion, finely chopped

175g/6oz each, turnip, sweet potato and
   pumpkin, roughly diced

5ml/1 tsp dried marjoram

2.5ml/½ tsp ground ginger

1.5ml/¼ tsp ground cinnamon

15ml/1 tbsp chopped spring onion
   (scallions)

1 litre/1¾ pints/4 cups vegetable stock

30ml/2 tbsp flaked almonds

1 fresh chilli, seeded and chopped

5ml/1 tsp sugar

25g/1oz creamed coconut

salt and freshly ground black pepper

chopped fresh coriander (cilantro), to
   garnish (optional)

1 Melt the butter or margarine in a large, non-stick pan. Fry the onion for five minutes. Add the diced vegetables and fry for 3–4 minutes.

2 Add the marjoram, ginger, cinnamon, spring onion and salt and pepper to taste. Fry over a low heat for about 10 minutes, stirring frequently.

3 Add the vegetable stock, flaked almonds, chilli and sugar and stir well to mix. Cover and simmer gently for 10–15 minutes until the vegetables are just tender.

4 Grate the creamed coconut into the soup and stir to mix. Spoon into warmed bowls, sprinkle with chopped coriander, if liked, and serve immediately.

Spicy Bean Soup

A filling soup made with two kinds of beans flavoured with cumin.

INGREDIENTS

Serves 6–8

175g/6oz/1 cup dried black beans, soaked
  overnight and drained
175g/6oz/1 cup dried kidney beans,
  soaked overnight and drained
2 bay leaves
90ml/6 tbsp coarse salt
30ml/2 tbsp olive or vegetable oil
3 carrots, chopped
1 onion, chopped
1 celery stick
1 garlic clove, crushed
5ml/1 tsp ground cumin
1.5–2.5ml/¼–½ tsp cayenne pepper
2.5ml/½ tsp dried oregano
50ml/2fl oz/¼ cup red wine
1.2 litres/2 pints/5 cups beef stock
250ml/8fl oz/1 cup water
salt and freshly ground black pepper

For the garnish
soured cream
chopped fresh coriander (cilantro)

1 Put the black beans and kidney
  beans in two separate pans
with cold water to cover and a
bay leaf in each. Boil rapidly for
10 minutes, then cover and
simmer for 20 minutes.

2 Add 45ml/3 tbsp coarse salt
  to each pan and continue
simmering for a further 30 minutes
until the beans are tender. Drain.

3 Heat the oil in a large
  flameproof casserole. Add the
carrots, onion, celery and garlic
and cook over a low heat for
8–10 minutes, stirring, until
softened. Stir in the cumin, cayenne,
oregano and salt to taste.

4 Add the wine, stock and water
  and stir to mix all the
ingredients together. Remove the
bay leaves from the cooked beans
and add the beans to the casserole.

5 Bring to the boil, reduce the
  heat, then cover and simmer
for about 20 minutes, stirring
occasionally.

6 Transfer half the soup
  (including most of the solids)
to a food processor or blender.
Process until smooth. Return to
the pan and stir to combine well.

7 Reheat the soup and adjust the
  seasoning to taste. Serve hot,
garnished with soured cream and
chopped coriander.

Black and White Bean Soup

V

Although this soup takes a while to prepare, the results are so stunning that it is well worth the effort.

INGREDIENTS

Serves 8

350g/12oz/2 cups dried black beans, soaked overnight and drained

2.4 litres/4¼ pints/10½ cups water

6 garlic cloves, crushed

350g/12oz/2 cups dried white beans, soaked overnight and drained

90ml/6 tbsp balsamic vinegar

4 jalapeño peppers, seeded and chopped

6 spring onions (scallions), finely chopped

juice of 1 lime

50ml/2fl oz/¼ cup olive oil

15g/½ oz/¼ cup chopped fresh coriander (cilantro), plus extra to garnish

salt and freshly ground black pepper

1 Place the black beans in a large pan with half the water and garlic. Bring to the boil. Reduce the heat to low, cover the pan, and simmer for about 1½ hours until the beans are soft.

2 Meanwhile, put the white beans in another pan with the remaining water and garlic. Bring to the boil, cover the pan and simmer for 1 hour or until soft.

3 Purée the cooked white beans in a food processor or blender. Stir in the vinegar, jalapeños, and half the spring onions. Return to the pan and reheat gently.

4 Purée the cooked black beans in the food processor or blender. Return to the pan and stir in the lime juice, olive oil, coriander and remaining spring onions. Reheat gently.

5 Season both soups with salt and freshly ground black pepper. To serve, place a ladleful of each puréed soup in each soup bowl, side by side. Swirl the two soups together with a cocktail stick or skewer. Garnish with fresh coriander and serve.

Plantain and Corn Soup

Here the sweetness of the corn and plantains is offset by a little chilli to create an unusual soup.

INGREDIENTS

Serves 4

25g/1oz/2 tbsp butter or margarine

1 onion, finely chopped

1 garlic clove, crushed

275g/10oz yellow plantains, peeled and sliced

1 large tomato, peeled and chopped

175g/6oz/1 cup sweetcorn kernels

5ml/1 tsp dried tarragon, crushed

900ml/1½ pints/3¾ cups vegetable or chicken stock

1 fresh green chilli, seeded and chopped

a pinch of freshly grated nutmeg

salt and freshly ground black pepper

1 Melt the butter or margarine in a pan over a moderate heat, add the onion and garlic and fry for a few minutes until the onion is soft.

2 Add the plantains, tomato and sweetcorn kernels, and cook for a further 5 minutes.

3 Add the tarragon, stock, green chilli and salt and freshly ground black pepper, then simmer for 10 minutes or until the plantain is tender. Stir in the grated nutmeg and serve at once.

Groundnut Soup

Groundnuts (or peanuts) are widely used in sauces in African cooking. You'll find groundnut paste in health food shops – it makes a wonderfully rich soup – but you could use peanut butter instead if you prefer.

INGREDIENTS

Serves 4

45ml/3 tbsp groundnut paste or peanut butter

1.5 litres/2½ pints/6¼ cups stock or water

30ml/2 tbsp tomato purée

1 onion, chopped

2 slices fresh root ginger

1.5ml/¼ tsp dried thyme

1 bay leaf

chilli powder

225g/8oz white yam, diced

10 small okras, trimmed (optional)

salt

1 Place the groundnut paste or peanut butter in a bowl, add 300ml/½ pint/1¼ cups of the stock or water and the tomato purée and blend together to make a smooth paste.

2 Spoon the nut mixture into a pan and add the onion, ginger, thyme, bay leaf, chilli powder and salt to taste and the remaining stock.

3 Heat gently until simmering, then cook for 1 hour, whisking from time to time to prevent the nut mixture sticking.

4 Add the white yam, cook for a further 10 minutes, and then add the okra, if using, and simmer until both vegetables are tender. Serve at once.

Spicy Chicken and Mushroom Soup

This creamy chicken soup makes a hearty meal. Serve it piping hot with fresh garlic bread.

Serves 4

75g/3oz/6 tbsp unsalted (sweet) butter

2.5ml/½ tsp crushed garlic

5ml/1 tsp garam masala

5ml/1 tsp crushed black peppercorns

5ml/1 tsp salt

1.5ml/¼ tsp freshly grated nutmeg

225g/8oz chicken, skinned and boned

1 medium leek, sliced

75g/3oz/generous 1 cup mushrooms, sliced

50g/2oz/⅓ cup sweetcorn kernels

300ml/½ pint/1¼ cups water

250ml/8fl oz/1 cup single (light) cream

30ml/2 tbsp chopped fresh coriander (cilantro)

5ml/1 tsp crushed dried red chillies, to garnish (optional)

1 Melt the butter in a pan. Lower the heat, add the garlic and garam masala. Lower the heat even further and add the black peppercorns, salt and nutmeg.

2 Cut the chicken pieces into very fine strips and add to the pan with the leek, mushrooms and sweetcorn. Cook for 5 minutes until the chicken is cooked through, stirring constantly.

3 Remove from the heat and allow to cool slightly. Transfer three-quarters of the mixture into a food processor or blender. Add the water and process for about 1 minute.

4 Pour the resulting purée back into the pan with the rest of the mixture and bring to the boil over a medium heat. Lower the heat and stir in the cream.

5 Add the fresh coriander. Taste and adjust the seasoning. Serve hot, garnished with crushed red chillies, if liked.

Chicken and Almond Soup

This soup makes an excellent lunch or supper dish when served with naan bread.

INGREDIENTS

Serves 4

75g/3oz/6 tbsp unsalted (sweet) butter

1 medium leek, chopped

2.5ml/½ tsp shredded fresh root ginger

75g/3oz/¾ cup ground almonds

5ml/1 tsp salt

2.5ml/½ tsp crushed black peppercorns

1 fresh green chilli, chopped

1 medium carrot, sliced

50g/2oz/½ cup frozen peas

115g/4oz/1 cup chicken, skinned, boned
    and cubed

30ml/2 tbsp chopped fresh coriander
    (cilantro)

450ml/¾ pint/scant 2 cups water

250ml/8fl oz/1 cup single (light) cream

4 sprigs of fresh coriander (cilantro)

1 Melt the butter in a deep, round-bottomed pan, and sauté the leek and the ginger until soft but only just turning brown.

2 Lower the heat and add the ground almonds, salt, peppercorns, chilli, carrot, peas and chicken. Fry for about 10 minutes or until the chicken is completely cooked, stirring constantly. Add the chopped fresh coriander.

3 Remove from the heat and allow to cool slightly. Transfer the mixture to a food processor or blender and process for about 1½ minutes. Pour in the water and blend for a further 30 seconds.

4 Pour back into the pan and bring to the boil, stirring occasionally. Once it has boiled, lower the heat and gradually stir in the cream. Cook gently for a further 2 minutes, stirring from time to time. Serve garnished with the sprigs of coriander.

Seafood Laksa

For a delicious meal, serve creamy rice noodles in a spicy coconut-flavoured soup, topped with seafood. The soup base can be made in advance and refrigerated.

INGREDIENTS

Serves 4

4 fresh red chillies, seeded and roughly chopped
1 onion, roughly chopped
1 piece blacan, the size of a stock cube
1 lemon grass stalk, chopped
1 small piece fresh root ginger, peeled and roughly chopped
6 macadamia nuts or almonds
60ml/4 tbsp vegetable oil
5ml/1 tsp paprika
5ml/1 tsp ground turmeric
475ml/16fl oz/2 cups fish stock
600ml/1 pint/2½ cups coconut milk (creamed coconut)
a dash of fish sauce (*nam pla*), to taste
12 king prawns (shrimp), peeled and deveined
8 scallops
225g/8oz prepared squid, cut into rings
350g/12oz rice vermicelli or rice noodles, soaked in warm water until soft
salt and freshly ground black pepper
lime halves, to serve

For the garnish

¼ cucumber, cut into matchsticks
2 fresh red chillies, seeded and finely sliced
30ml/2 tbsp mint leaves
30ml/2 tbsp fried shallots or onions

1 In a blender or food processor, process the chillies, onion, blacan, lemon grass, ginger and nuts until smooth in texture.

2 Heat 45ml/3 tbsp of the oil in a large pan. Add the chilli paste and fry for 6 minutes. Stir in the paprika and turmeric and fry for about 2 minutes more.

3 Add the stock and the coconut milk to the pan. Bring to the boil, then simmer gently for 15–20 minutes. Season with fish sauce.

4 Season the seafood with salt and pepper. Fry quickly in the remaining oil for 2–3 minutes until cooked.

5 Add the noodles to the soup and heat through. Divide among individual serving bowls. Place the fried seafood on top, then garnish with the cucumber, chillies, mint and fried shallots or onions. Serve with the limes.

Curried Salmon Soup

*A hint of mild curry paste really
enhances the flavour of this soup.*

INGREDIENTS

Serves 4

50g/2oz/4 tbsp butter

225g/8oz onions, roughly chopped

10ml/2 tsp mild curry paste

475ml/16fl oz/2 cups water

150ml/¼ pint/⅔ cup white wine

300ml/½ pint/1¼ cups double
   (heavy) cream

50g/2oz/½ cup creamed coconut, grated

350g/12oz potatoes, finely chopped

450g/1lb salmon fillet, skinned and cut
   into bite-size pieces

60ml/4 tbsp chopped fresh flat-leaf parsley

salt and freshly ground black pepper

1 Melt the butter in a large pan,
add the onions and cook over
a low heat for about 3–4 minutes
until beginning to soften. Add
the curry paste and cook for
1 minute further.

2 Add the water, wine, cream,
creamed coconut and a little
seasoning. Bring to the boil,
stirring, until the coconut has
dissolved smoothly.

3 Add the potatoes to the pan
and simmer, covered, for
about 15 minutes, or until they are
almost tender. Do not allow them
to break down into the mixture.

4 Stir in the fish gently so as not
to break it up. Simmer for
2–3 minutes until just tender. Add
the parsley and adjust the
seasoning. Serve immediately.

Smoked Cod and Okra Soup

The inspiration for this soup came from a Ghanaian recipe for okra soup. Here it is enhanced by the addition of smoked fish.

INGREDIENTS

Serves 4

2 green bananas

50g/2oz/4 tbsp butter or margarine

1 onion, finely chopped

2 tomatoes, peeled and finely chopped

115g/4oz okra, trimmed

225g/8oz smoked cod fillet, cut into
    bite-size pieces

900ml/1½ pints/3¾ cups fish stock

1 fresh chilli, seeded and chopped

salt and freshly ground black pepper

sprigs of fresh parsley, to garnish

3 Add the cod, fish stock, chilli and seasoning. Bring to the boil, then reduce the heat and simmer for about 20 minutes or until the cod is cooked through and flakes easily.

4 Peel the cooked bananas and cut into slices. Stir into the soup, heat through for a few minutes and ladle into soup bowls. Garnish with parsley and serve.

1 Slit the skins of the green bananas and place in a large pan. Cover with water, bring to the boil and cook over a moderate heat for 25 minutes until the bananas are tender. Transfer to a plate and leave to cool.

2 Melt the butter or margarine in a large pan and sauté the onion for about 5 minutes until soft. Stir in the chopped tomatoes and okra and fry gently for a further 10 minutes.

Mulligatawny Soup

Mulligatawny *(which literally means "pepper water") was introduced into England in the late eighteenth century by members of the colonial services returning home from India.*

INGREDIENTS

Serves 4

50g/2oz/4 tbsp butter or 60ml/4 tbsp oil

2 large chicken joints (about 350g/
    12oz each)

1 onion, chopped

1 carrot, chopped

1 small turnip, chopped

about 15ml/1 tbsp curry powder, to taste

4 cloves

6 black peppercorns, lightly crushed

50g/2oz/¼ cup lentils

900ml/1½ pints/3¾ cups chicken stock

40g/1½ oz/¼ cup sultanas

salt and freshly ground black pepper

1 Melt the butter or heat the oil in a large pan, then brown the chicken over a brisk heat. Transfer the chicken to a plate and set aside.

2 Add the onion, carrot and turnip to the pan and cook, stirring occasionally, until lightly coloured. Stir in the curry powder, cloves and crushed peppercorns and cook for 1–2 minutes, then add the lentils.

3 Pour the stock into the pan, bring to the boil, then add the sultanas, the chicken and any juices from the plate. Cover and simmer gently for about 1¼ hours.

> ### COOK'S TIP
> ❦
> Choose red split lentils for the best colour, although either green or brown lentils could also be used.

4 Remove the chicken from the pan and discard the skin and bones. Chop the flesh, return to the soup and reheat. Check the seasoning before serving the soup piping hot.

Squash, Bacon and Swiss Cheese Soup

This is a lightly spiced squash soup, enriched with plenty of creamy melting cheese.

Serves 4

900g/2lb butternut squash
225g/8oz smoked back bacon
15ml/1 tbsp oil
225g/8oz onions, roughly chopped
2 garlic cloves, crushed
10ml/2 tsp ground cumin
15ml/1 tbsp ground coriander
275g/10oz potatoes, cut into small chunks
900ml/1½ pints/3¾ cups vegetable stock
10ml/2 tsp cornflour (corn starch)
30ml/2 tbsp crème fraîche
Tabasco sauce, to taste
salt and freshly ground black pepper
175g/6oz/1½ cups Gruyère cheese, grated,
  to serve
crusty bread to serve

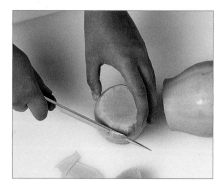

1 Cut the squash into large pieces. Using a sharp knife, carefully remove the skin, wasting as little flesh as possible.

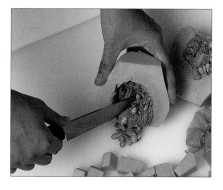

2 Scoop out and discard the seeds. Chop the squash into small chunks. Remove all the fat from the bacon and roughly chop it into small pieces.

3 Heat the oil in a large pan and cook the onions and garlic for 3 minutes, or until beginning to soften.

4 Add the bacon and cook for about 3 minutes. Stir in the spices and cook on a low heat for a further minute.

5 Add the chopped squash, potatoes and stock. Bring to the boil and simmer for 15 minutes, or until the squash and potatoes are tender.

6 Blend the cornflour with 30ml/2 tbsp water and add to the soup with the crème fraîche. Bring to the boil and simmer, uncovered, for 3 minutes. Adjust the seasoning and add Tabasco sauce to taste.

7 Ladle the soup into warm bowls and sprinkle the cheese on top. Serve immediately with crusty bread to scoop up the melted cheese.

COOK'S TIP

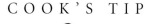

Pumpkin can be used instead of butternut squash and is equally delicious.

Thai-style Chicken Soup

A fragrant blend of coconut milk,
lemon grass, ginger and lime.

INGREDIENTS

Serves 4

5ml/1 tsp oil

1–2 fresh red chillies, seeded and chopped

2 garlic cloves, crushed

1 large leek, finely sliced

600ml/1 pint/2½ cups chicken stock

400ml/14fl oz/1⅔ cups coconut milk
(coconut cream)

450g/1lb skinless boneless chicken thighs,
cut into bite-size pieces

30ml/2 tbsp Thai fish (*nam pla*) sauce

1 lemon grass stalk, split

2.5cm/1in piece fresh root ginger, peeled
and finely chopped

5ml/1 tsp sugar

4 kaffir lime leaves (optional)

75g/3oz/¾ cup frozen peas, thawed

45ml/3 tbsp chopped fresh coriander
(cilantro)

3 Add the chicken, fish sauce, lemon grass, ginger, sugar and lime leaves, if using. Lower the heat and simmer, covered, for 15 minutes until the chicken is tender, stirring occasionally.

4 Add the peas and cook for a further 3 minutes. Remove the lemon grass and stir in the coriander just before serving.

1 Heat the oil in a large pan and cook the chillies and garlic for about 2 minutes. Add the leek and cook for a further 2 minutes.

2 Stir in the stock and coconut milk and bring to the boil over a medium-high heat.

Thai Chicken Soup

Enjoy the characteristic Thai flavours of garlic, coconut, lemon, and chilli with this soup.

INGREDIENTS

Serves 4

15ml/1 tbsp vegetable oil

1 garlic clove, finely chopped

2 skinless, boneless chicken breasts (175g/6oz each) chopped

2.5ml/½ tsp ground turmeric

1.5ml/¼ tsp hot chilli powder

75g/3oz/½ cup creamed coconut (coconut cream)

900ml/1½ pints/3¾ cups hot chicken stock

30ml/2 tbsp lemon or lime juice

30ml/2 tbsp crunchy peanut butter

50g/2oz/1 cup thread egg noodles, broken into small pieces

15ml/1 tbsp chopped spring onions (scallions)

15ml/1 tbsp chopped fresh coriander (cilantro)

salt and freshly ground black pepper

desiccated (dry unsweetened, shredded) coconut, to garnish

finely chopped fresh red chilli, to garnish

1 Heat the oil. Fry the garlic for 1 minute. Add the chicken and spices. Stir-fry for 3–4 minutes.

2 Crumble the creamed coconut into the hot chicken stock and stir until dissolved. Pour on to the chicken breasts and add the lemon or lime juice, peanut butter and thread egg noodles.

3 Cover the pan and simmer for 15 minutes. Add the spring onions and fresh coriander, season well with salt and freshly ground black pepper and cook gently for a further 5 minutes.

4 Meanwhile, heat the desiccated coconut and chilli in a small frying pan for 2 minutes, stirring frequently, until the coconut is lightly browned.

5 Pour the soup into bowls and serve sprinkled with the dry-fried coconut and chilli.

Chicken, Tomato and Christophene Soup

Chicken breasts and smoked haddock take on the flavours of herbs and spices to produce this well-flavoured soup.

INGREDIENTS

Serves 4

225g/8oz skinless, boneless chicken
   breasts, diced
1 garlic clove, crushed
a pinch of freshly grated nutmeg
25g/1oz/2 tbsp butter or margarine
½ onion, finely chopped
15ml/1 tbsp tomato purée
400g/14oz can tomatoes, puréed
1.2 litres/2 pints/5 cups chicken stock
1 fresh chilli, seeded and chopped
1 christophene (chayote), peeled and
   diced (about 350g/12oz)
5ml/1 tsp dried oregano
2.5ml/½ tsp dried thyme
50g/2oz smoked haddock fillet, skinned
   and diced
salt and freshly ground black pepper
chopped fresh chives, to garnish

1 Dice the chicken, place in a bowl and season with salt, pepper, garlic and nutmeg. Mix well to flavour and then set aside for about 30 minutes.

2 Melt the butter or margarine in a large pan, add the chicken and sauté over a moderate heat for 5–6 minutes. Stir in the onion and fry gently for a further 5 minutes or until the onion is slightly softened.

3 Add the tomato purée, puréed tomatoes, stock, chilli, christophene and herbs. Bring to the boil, cover and simmer gently for 35 minutes or until the christophene is tender.

4 Add the smoked fish and simmer for a further 5 minutes or until the fish is cooked through. Adjust the seasoning and pour into warmed soup bowls. Garnish with a scattering of chopped fresh chives and serve piping hot.

Beef Chilli Soup

This is a hearty dish based on a traditional chilli recipe. It is ideal served with fresh, crusty bread as a warming start to any meal.

Serves 4

15ml/1 tbsp oil
1 onion, chopped
175g/6oz/¾ cup minced (ground) beef
2 garlic cloves, chopped
1 fresh red chilli, sliced
25g/1oz/¼ cup plain (all-purpose) flour
400g/14oz can chopped tomatoes
600ml/1 pint/2½ cups beef stock
225g/8oz/2 cups canned kidney beans, drained
30ml/2 tbsp chopped fresh parsley
salt and freshly ground black pepper
crusty bread, to serve

1 Heat the oil in a large pan. Fry the onion and minced beef for 5 minutes until brown and sealed.

2 Add the garlic, chilli and flour. Cook for 1 minute. Add the tomatoes and pour in the stock. Bring to the boil.

3 Stir in the kidney beans and add salt and pepper to taste. Cook for 20 minutes.

4 Add the chopped parsley, reserving a little to garnish the finished dish. Pour the soup into warm bowls, sprinkle with the reserved parsley and serve with crusty bread.

COOK'S TIP

For a milder flavour, remove the seeds from the chilli after slicing.

Chiang Mai Noodle Soup

A signature dish of the city of Chiang Mai, this delicious noodle soup has Burmese origins.

INGREDIENTS

Serves 4–6

600ml/1 pint/2½ cups coconut milk (coconut cream)
30ml/2 tbsp red curry paste
5ml/1 tsp ground turmeric
450g/1lb chicken thighs, boned and cut into bite-size chunks
600ml/1 pint/2½ cups chicken stock
60ml/4 tbsp fish (*nam pla*) sauce
15ml/1 tbsp dark soy sauce
juice of ½–1 lime
450g/1lb fresh egg noodles, blanched briefly in boiling water
salt and freshly ground black pepper

For the garnish

3 spring onions (scallions), chopped
4 fresh red chillies, chopped
4 shallots, chopped
60ml/4 tbsp sliced pickled mustard leaves, rinsed
30ml/2 tbsp fried sliced garlic
fresh coriander (cilantro) leaves
4 fried noodle nests (optional)

1 Pour about one-third of the coconut milk into a large pan and bring to the boil, stirring often with a wooden spoon until it separates.

2 Add the curry paste and ground turmeric, stir to mix together and cook until fragrant.

3 Add the chicken and stir-fry for about 2 minutes, ensuring that all the chunks are coated with the paste.

4 Add the remaining coconut milk, chicken stock, fish sauce and soy sauce. Season to taste and simmer gently for 7–10 minutes. Remove from the heat and stir in the lime juice.

5 Reheat the noodles in boiling water, drain and divide between individual bowls. Divide the chicken between the bowls and ladle in the hot soup. Top each serving of soup with a few of each of the garnishes.

Moroccan Harira

This substantial meat and vegetable soup is eaten during Ramadan, when the Muslim population fasts between sunrise and sunset.

INGREDIENTS

Serves 4

25g/1oz/2 tbsp butter
225g/8oz lamb, cut into 1cm/½in pieces
1 onion, chopped
450g/1lb well-flavoured tomatoes
60ml/4 tbsp chopped fresh coriander
   (cilantro)
30ml/2 tbsp chopped fresh parsley
2.5ml/½ tsp ground turmeric
2.5ml/½ tsp ground cinnamon
50g/2oz/¼ cup red lentils
75g/3oz/½ cup chickpeas, soaked
   overnight
600ml/1 pint/2½ cups water
4 baby onions or small shallots, peeled
25g/1oz/¼ cup soup noodles
salt and freshly ground black pepper

For the garnish
chopped fresh coriander (cilantro)
lemon slices
ground cinnamon

1 Heat the butter in a large pan or flameproof casserole and fry the lamb and onion for 5 minutes, stirring frequently.

2 Peel the tomatoes, if you wish, by plunging them into boiling water to loosen the skins. Wait for them to cool a little before peeling off the skins. Then cut them into quarters and add to the lamb with the herbs and spices.

3 Rinse the lentils under cold running water and drain the chickpeas. Add both to the pan with the water. Season with salt and pepper. Bring to the boil, cover and simmer gently for 1½ hours.

4 Add the baby onions or small shallots and cook for a further 30 minutes. Add the noodles 5 minutes before the end of the cooking time. Serve the soup when the noodles are tender, garnished with the coriander, lemon slices and cinnamon.

Vegetable Broth with Minced Beef

This is a veritable cornucopia of flavours, combining to produce a rich and satisfying broth.

INGREDIENTS

Serves 6

30ml/2 tbsp groundnut (peanut) oil
115g/4oz finely minced (ground) beef
1 large onion, grated or finely chopped
1 garlic clove, crushed
1–2 fresh chillies, seeded and chopped
1cm/½ in cube terasi, prepared
3 macadamia nuts or 6 almonds,
    finely ground
1 carrot, finely grated
5ml/1 tsp brown sugar
1 litre/1¾ pints/4 cups chicken stock
50g/2oz dried shrimps, soaked in warm
    water for 10 minutes
225g/8oz spinach, finely shredded
8 baby sweetcorn, sliced, or 200g/7oz
    canned sweetcorn kernels
1 large tomato, chopped
juice of ½ lemon
salt

1 Heat the oil in a pan. Add the beef, onion and garlic and cook, stirring, until the meat changes colour.

2 Add the chillies, terasi, macadamia nuts or almonds, carrot, sugar and salt to taste.

3 Add the stock and bring gently to the boil. Reduce the heat to a simmer and then add the soaked shrimps, with their soaking liquid. Simmer for about 10 minutes.

4 A few minutes before serving, add the spinach, sweetcorn, tomato and lemon juice. Simmer for 2 minutes, to heat through. Do not overcook at this stage because this will spoil both the appearance and the taste of the end result. Serve immediately.

COOK'S TIP

To make this broth very hot and spicy, add the seeds from the chillies.

Beef and Herb Soup with Yogurt

This classic Iranian soup, aashe maste, *is full of invigorating herbs and is a popular cold-weather dish.*

Serves 4

2 large onions

30ml/2 tbsp oil

15ml/1 tbsp ground turmeric

90g/3½ oz/scant ½ cup yellow split peas

1.2 litres/2 pints/5 cups water

225g/8oz minced (ground) beef

200g/7oz/1 cup rice

45ml/3 tbsp each chopped fresh parsley,
    coriander (cilantro) and chives

15g/½ oz/1 tbsp butter

1 large garlic clove, finely chopped

60ml/4 tbsp chopped fresh mint

2–3 saffron threads dissolved in
    15ml/1 tbsp boiling water (optional)

salt and freshly ground black pepper

natural (US plain) yogurt and naan bread,
    to serve

1 Chop one of the onions. Heat the oil in a large pan and fry the chopped onion until golden brown. Add the turmeric, split peas and water, bring to the boil, then reduce the heat and simmer for 20 minutes.

2 Grate the other onion into a bowl, add the minced beef and seasoning and mix well. Using your hands, form the mixture into small balls about the size of walnuts. Carefully add to the pan and simmer for 10 minutes.

3 Add the rice, parsley, coriander and chives. Simmer for about 30 minutes until the rice is tender, stirring frequently.

4 Melt the butter in a small pan and gently fry the garlic. Stir in the mint and sprinkle over the soup with the saffron, if using.

5 Spoon the soup into warmed serving dishes and serve with yogurt and naan bread.

COOK'S TIP

Fresh spinach is also delicious in this soup. Add 50g/2oz finely chopped spinach leaves along with the parsley, coriander and chives.

CHUNKY SOUPS

Chunky Bean and Vegetable Soup

V

A substantial soup, not unlike minestrone, using a selection of vegetables, with cannellini beans for extra protein and fibre. Serve with a hunk of wholegrain bread.

INGREDIENTS

Serves 4

30ml/2 tbsp olive oil

2 celery sticks, chopped

2 leeks, sliced

3 carrots, sliced

2 garlic cloves, crushed

400g/14oz can chopped tomatoes
  with basil

1.2 litres/2 pints/5 cups vegetable stock

400g/14oz can cannellini beans (or mixed
  pulses), drained

15ml/1 tbsp pesto sauce

salt and freshly ground black pepper

Parmesan cheese shavings, to serve

1 Heat the olive oil in a large pan. Add the celery, leeks, carrots and garlic and cook gently for about 5 minutes until they have softened.

COOK'S TIP

Extra vegetables can be added to the soup to make it even more substantial. For example, add some thinly sliced courgettes (zucchini) or finely shredded cabbage for the last 5 minutes of the cooking time. Or, stir in some small wholewheat pasta shapes. Add them at the same time as the tomatoes, as they will take 10–15 minutes to cook.

2 Stir in the tomatoes and stock. Bring to the boil, then cover and cook gently for 15 minutes.

3 Stir in the beans and pesto, with salt and pepper to taste. Heat through for a further 5 minutes. Serve in heated bowls, sprinkled with shavings of Parmesan cheese.

Broad Bean and Rice Soup

This thick soup makes the most of fresh broad (fava) beans while they are in season. It works well with frozen beans for the rest of the year.

INGREDIENTS

Serves 4

1kg/2¼lb broad (fava) beans in their
   pods, or 400g/14oz shelled frozen broad
   (fava) beans, thawed
90ml/6 tbsp olive oil
1 medium onion, finely chopped
2 medium tomatoes, peeled and
   finely chopped
225g/8oz/1 cup arborio or other
   non-parboiled rice
25g/1oz/2 tbsp butter
1 litre/1¾ pints/4 cups boiling water
salt and freshly ground black pepper
grated Parmesan cheese, to
   serve (optional)

1 Shell the beans if they are fresh. Bring a large pan of water to the boil and blanch the beans, fresh or frozen, for 4 minutes. Rinse under cold water and peel off the skins.

2 Heat the oil in a large pan. Add the onion and cook over low to moderate heat until it softens. Stir in the beans and cook for about 5 minutes, stirring to coat them with the oil.

3 Season with salt and pepper. Add the tomatoes and cook for 5 minutes more, stirring often. Add the rice and cook for a further 1–2 minutes, stirring constantly.

4 Add the butter and stir until it melts. Pour in the water, a little at a time. Adjust the seasoning to taste. Continue cooking until the rice is tender. Serve with grated Parmesan, if liked.

Fresh Tomato and Bean Soup

This is a rich, chunky tomato soup, best served with olive ciabatta.

INGREDIENTS

Serves 4

900g/2lb ripe plum tomatoes
30ml/2 tbsp olive oil
275g/10oz onions, roughly chopped
2 garlic cloves, crushed
900ml/1½ pints/3¾ cups vegetable stock
30ml/2 tbsp sun-dried tomato purée
   (paste)
10ml/2 tsp paprika
15ml/1 tbsp cornflour (cornstarch)
425g/15oz can cannellini beans, drained
30ml/2 tbsp chopped fresh
   coriander (cilantro)
salt and freshly ground black pepper
olive ciabatta bread, to serve

1 First, peel the tomatoes. Using a sharp knife, make a small cross in each one and place in a bowl. Pour over boiling water to cover and leave to stand for 30–60 seconds.

2 Drain the tomatoes and, when they are cool enough to handle, peel off the skins. Quarter them and then cut each piece in half again.

3 Heat the oil in a large pan and cook the onions and garlic for 3 minutes or until just beginning to soften.

4 Add the tomatoes to the onions and stir in the stock, sun-dried tomato purée and paprika. Season with a little salt and pepper. Bring to the boil and simmer for 10 minutes.

5 Mix the cornflour to a paste with 30ml/2 tbsp water. Stir the beans into the soup with the cornflour paste. Cook for a further 5 minutes.

6 Adjust the seasoning and stir in the chopped coriander just before serving with olive ciabatta.

V

Pistou

Serve this delicious vegetable soup with a sun-dried tomato pesto and fresh Parmesan cheese.

INGREDIENTS

Serves 4

1 courgette (zucchini), diced

1 small potato, diced

1 shallot, chopped

1 carrot, diced

225g/8oz can chopped tomatoes

1.2 litres/2 pints/5 cups vegetable stock

50g/2oz green beans, cut into 1cm/½in lengths

50g/2oz/½ cup petits pois (baby peas)

50g/2oz/½ cup small pasta shapes

60–90ml/4–6 tbsp pesto, either home-made or ready-made

15ml/1 tbsp sun-dried tomato purée (paste)

salt and freshly ground black pepper

grated Parmesan cheese, to serve

1 Place the courgette, potato, shallot, carrot and tomatoes in a large pan. Add the vegetable stock and season with salt and pepper. Bring to the boil, then cover and simmer for 20 minutes.

2 Add the green beans, petits pois and pasta shapes. Cook for a further 10 minutes, until the pasta is tender.

3 Taste the soup and adjust the seasoning as necessary. Ladle the soup into individual bowls. Mix together the pesto and sun-dried tomato purée, and stir a spoonful into each serving.

4 Hand around a bowl of grated Parmesan cheese for sprinkling into each bowl.

Ribollita

Ribollita is rather like minestrone, but includes beans instead of pasta. In Italy it is traditionally served ladled over bread and a rich green vegetable, although you could omit this for a lighter version.

INGREDIENTS

Serves 6–8

45ml/3 tbsp olive oil

2 onions, chopped

2 carrots, sliced

4 garlic cloves, crushed

2 celery sticks, finely sliced

1 fennel bulb, trimmed and chopped

2 large courgettes (zucchini), thinly sliced

400g/14oz can chopped tomatoes

30ml/2 tbsp pesto, either home-made or
    ready-made

900ml/1½ pints/3¾ cups vegetable stock

400g/14oz can haricot (navy) or borlotti
    beans, drained

salt and freshly ground black pepper

To serve

450g/1lb young spinach

15ml/1 tbsp extra virgin olive oil, plus
    extra for drizzling

6–8 slices white bread

Parmesan cheese shavings (optional)

1 Heat the oil in a large pan. Add the onions, carrots, garlic, celery and fennel and fry gently for 10 minutes. Add the courgette slices and fry for a further 2 minutes.

2 Add the chopped tomatoes, pesto, stock and beans and bring to the boil. Reduce the heat, cover and simmer gently for 25–30 minutes until all the vegetables are tender. Season with salt and freshly ground black pepper to taste.

3 To serve, fry the spinach in the oil for 2 minutes or until wilted. Spoon over the bread in soup bowls, then ladle the soup over the spinach. Serve with extra olive oil for drizzling on to the soup and Parmesan cheese to sprinkle on top, if liked.

V

Italian Rocket and Potato Soup

This filling and hearty soup is based on an Italian peasant recipe. Baby spinach leaves make an equally delicious alternative to rocket.

INGREDIENTS

Serves 4

900g/2lb new potatoes

900ml/1½ pints/3¾ cups well-flavoured
  vegetable stock

1 medium carrot

115g/4oz rocket (arugula)

2.5ml/½ tsp cayenne pepper

½ loaf stale ciabatta bread, torn into
  chunks

4 garlic cloves, thinly sliced

60ml/4 tbsp olive oil

salt and freshly ground black pepper

3 Add the cayenne pepper, plus salt and black pepper to taste, then add the chunks of bread. Remove the pan from the heat, cover and leave to stand for about 10 minutes.

4 Meanwhile, sauté the garlic in the olive oil until golden brown. Pour the soup into bowls, add a little of the sautéed garlic to each bowl and serve.

1 Dice the potatoes, then place them in a pan with the stock and a little salt. Bring to the boil and simmer for 10 minutes.

2 Dice the carrot and add to the potatoes and stock. Tear the rocket leaves and add to the pan. Simmer for a further 15 minutes, until the vegetables are tender.

Czech Fish Soup with Dumplings

Use a variety of whatever fish is available in this Czech soup, such as perch, catfish, cod or snapper. The basis of the dumplings is the same whether you use semolina or flour.

INGREDIENTS

Serves 4–8

3 rindless bacon rashers (strips), diced

675g/1½ lb assorted fresh fish, skinned, boned and diced

15ml/1 tbsp paprika, plus extra to garnish

1.5 litres/2½ pints/6¼ cups fish stock or water

3 firm tomatoes, peeled and chopped

4 waxy potatoes, peeled and grated

5–10ml/1–2 tsp chopped fresh marjoram, plus extra to garnish

For the dumplings

75g/3oz/½ cup semolina or flour

1 egg, beaten

45ml/3 tbsp milk or water

generous pinch of salt

15ml/1 tbsp chopped fresh parsley

1 Dry fry the diced bacon in a large pan until pale golden brown, then add the pieces of assorted fish. Fry for 2 minutes, taking care not to break up the pieces of fish.

2 Sprinkle in the paprika, pour in the fish stock or water, bring to the boil and simmer for 10 minutes.

3 Stir the tomatoes, grated potato and marjoram into the pan. Cook for 10 minutes, stirring occasionally.

4 Meanwhile, make the dumplings by mixing all the ingredients together, then leave to stand, covered with clear film for 5–10 minutes.

5 Drop spoonfuls of the dumpling mixture into the soup and cook for 10 minutes. Serve hot with a little marjoram and paprika.

Lentil and Pasta Soup

V

This rustic soup is a filling lunch and goes well with granary or crusty Italian bread.

INGREDIENTS

Serves 4–6

175g/6oz/¾ cup brown lentils

3 garlic cloves

1 litre/1¾ pints/4 cups water

45ml/3 tbsp olive oil

25g/1oz/2 tbsp butter

1 onion, finely chopped

2 celery sticks, finely chopped

30ml/2 tbsp sun-dried tomato purée
 (paste)

1.75 litres/3 pints/7½ cups vegetable stock

a few fresh marjoram leaves, plus extra
 to garnish

a few fresh basil leaves

leaves from 1 sprig of fresh thyme

50g/2oz/½ cup small pasta shapes,
 such as tubetti

salt and freshly ground black pepper

1 Put the lentils in a large pan. Smash one of the garlic cloves (there's no need to peel it first) and add it to the lentils. Pour in the water and bring to the boil. Lower the heat to a gentle simmer and cook for about 20 minutes, stirring occasionally, until the lentils are just tender.

2 Tip the lentils into a sieve, remove the cooked garlic clove and set it aside.

3 Rinse the lentils under cold running water, then leave them to drain. Heat 30ml/2 tbsp of the oil with half of the butter in a large pan. Add the onion and celery and cook over a low heat, stirring frequently, for 5–7 minutes until softened.

COOK'S TIP

Use green lentils instead of brown, if you like, but the orange or red ones are not so good for this soup because they tend to go mushy.

4 Crush the remaining garlic and peel and mash the reserved cooked garlic clove. Add to the vegetables with the remaining oil, the tomato purée and lentils. Stir, then add the stock, herbs and salt and pepper to taste. Bring to the boil, stirring. Simmer the soup gently for 30 minutes, stirring occasionally.

5 Add the pasta and bring to the boil, stirring. Simmer, stirring frequently, for 7–8 minutes or according to the instructions on the packet, until the pasta is *al dente*. Add the remaining butter and adjust the seasoning. Serve hot in warmed bowls, garnished with marjoram leaves.

Lentil Soup with Rosemary

A classic rustic Italian soup flavoured with rosemary, this is delicious served with garlic bread.

INGREDIENTS

Serves 4

225g/8oz/1 cup dried green or
    brown lentils
45ml/3 tbsp extra virgin olive oil
3 rindless streaky (fatty) bacon rashers
    (strips), cut into small dice
1 onion, finely chopped
2 celery sticks, finely chopped
2 carrots, finely chopped
2 sprigs of fresh rosemary, finely chopped
2 bay leaves
400g/14oz can plum tomatoes
1.75 litres/3 pints/7½ cups vegetable stock
salt and freshly ground black pepper
fresh bay leaves and sprigs of fresh
    rosemary, to garnish

1 Place the lentils in a bowl and cover with cold water. Leave to soak for at least 2 hours. Rinse and drain well.

2 Heat the oil in a large pan. Add the bacon and cook for about 3 minutes, then stir in the onion and cook for 5 minutes until softened. Stir in the celery, carrots, rosemary, bay leaves and lentils. Toss over the heat for 1 minute until thoroughly coated in the oil.

3 Tip in the tomatoes and stock, and bring to the boil. Lower the heat, half-cover the pan and simmer for about 1 hour until the lentils are perfectly tender.

4 Remove the bay leaves, add salt and freshly ground black pepper to taste and serve with a garnish of fresh bay leaves and sprigs of rosemary.

COOK'S TIP

Look for the small
green lentils in Italian groceries
or delicatessens.

Tiny Pasta in Broth

In Italy this soup is often served with bread for a light supper.

Serves 4

1.2 litres/2 pints/5 cups beef stock

75g/3oz/³⁄₄ cup small soup pasta, such as stellette

2 pieces bottled roasted red (bell) pepper (about 50g/2oz)

salt and freshly ground black pepper

grated Parmesan cheese, to serve

1 Bring the beef stock to the boil in a large pan. Add salt and pepper to taste, then drop in the soup pasta. Stir well and bring the stock back to the boil.

2 Lower the heat to a simmer and cook for 7–8 minutes or according to the packet instructions, until the pasta is *al dente*. Stir often during cooking to prevent the pasta shapes from sticking.

3 Drain the pieces of bottled roasted pepper and dice them finely. Place them in the bottom of four warmed soup plates, and set them aside.

4 Taste the soup and adjust the seasoning. Ladle into the soup plates and serve immediately, with grated Parmesan handed round separately.

Little Stuffed Hats in Broth

This soup is served in northern Italy on Santo Stefano (St Stephen's Day – 26 December) and on New Year's Day. It makes a welcome change from all the special celebration food, the day before. It is traditionally made with the Christmas capon carcass, but chicken stock works equally well.

Serves 4

1.2 litres/2 pints/5 cups chicken stock

90–115g/3¹⁄₂–4oz/1 cup fresh or dried cappelletti

30ml/2 tbsp dry white wine (optional)

about 15ml/1 tbsp finely chopped fresh flat leaf parsley (optional)

salt and freshly ground black pepper

about 30ml/2 tbsp grated Parmesan cheese, to serve

1 Pour the chicken stock into a large pan and bring to the boil. Add a little salt and pepper to taste, then drop in the pasta.

2 Stir well and bring back to the boil. Lower the heat to a simmer and cook according to the instructions on the packet, until the pasta is *al dente*. Stir frequently during cooking to ensure the pasta cooks evenly.

3 Swirl in the wine and parsley, if using, then taste and adjust the seasoning. Ladle into four warmed soup plates, then sprinkle with grated Parmesan. Serve immediately.

COOK'S TIP

Cappelletti is just another name for tortellini, which come from Romagna. You can either buy them ready-made or make your own.

Chickpea and Spinach Soup with Garlic

V

This delicious, thick and creamy soup is richly flavoured and perfect for vegetarians.

INGREDIENTS

Serves 4

30ml/2 tbsp olive oil

4 garlic cloves, crushed

1 onion, roughly chopped

10ml/2 tsp ground cumin

10ml/2 tsp ground coriander

1.2 litres/2 pints/5 cups vegetable stock

350g/12oz potatoes, finely chopped

425g/15oz can chickpeas, drained

15ml/1 tbsp cornflour (cornstarch)

150ml/¼ pint/⅔ cup double (heavy) cream

30ml/2 tbsp light tahini

200g/7oz spinach, shredded

cayenne pepper

salt and freshly ground black pepper

2 Stir in the ground cumin and coriander and cook for
1 minute. Add the stock and potatoes. Bring to the boil and simmer for 10 minutes.

3 Add the chickpeas and simmer for a further 5 minutes or until the potatoes are just tender.

4 Blend together the cornflour, cream, tahini and plenty of seasoning. Stir into the soup with the spinach. Bring to the boil, stirring, and simmer for a further 2 minutes. Adjust the seasoning with salt, pepper and cayenne pepper to taste. Serve sprinkled with a little extra cayenne pepper.

1 Heat the oil in a large pan and cook the garlic and onion for about 5 minutes or until the onion is softened and golden brown.

COOK'S TIP

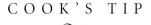

Tahini is sesame seed paste and is available from many health food shops.

Eastern European Chickpea Soup

V

Chickpeas form part of the staple diet in the Balkans. It is a hearty and satisfying dish.

INGREDIENTS

Serves 4–6

500g/1¼ lb/5 cups chickpeas,
   soaked overnight

2 litres/3½ pints/9 cups vegetable stock

3 large waxy potatoes, cut into
   bitesize chunks

50ml/2fl oz/¼ cup olive oil

225g/8oz spinach leaves

salt and freshly ground black pepper

spicy sausage, cooked (optional)

1 Drain the chickpeas and rinse under cold water. Place in a large pan with the vegetable stock. Bring to the boil, then reduce the heat and cook gently for about 1 hour.

2 Add the potatoes, olive oil and salt and pepper to taste. Cook for 20 minutes until the potatoes are tender.

3 Add the spinach and sliced cooked sausage (if using) 5 minutes before the end of cooking. Serve the soup in individual warmed soup bowls.

Spiced Mussel Soup

Chunky and colourful, this Turkish fish soup is like a chowder in its consistency. It is flavoured with harissa sauce, which is more familiar in north African cookery.

INGREDIENTS

Serves 6

1.5kg/3–3½lb fresh mussels
150ml/¼ pint/⅔ cup white wine
30ml/2 tbsp olive oil
1 onion, finely chopped
2 garlic cloves, crushed
2 celery sticks, thinly sliced
bunch of spring onions (scallions),
    thinly sliced
1 potato, diced
7.5ml/1½ tsp harissa sauce
3 tomatoes, peeled and diced
45ml/3 tbsp chopped fresh parsley
freshly ground black pepper
thick natural (US plain) yogurt, to serve

1 Scrub the mussels; discard any damaged ones or open ones that do not close when tapped.

2 Bring the wine to the boil in a large pan. Add the mussels and cover with a lid. Cook for 4–5 minutes until the mussels have opened wide. Discard any mussels that remain closed. Drain the mussels, reserving the cooking liquid. Reserve a few mussels in their shells to use as a garnish and shell the rest.

3 Heat the oil in a pan and fry the onion, garlic, celery and spring onions for 5 minutes.

4 Add the shelled mussels, reserved liquid, potato, harissa sauce and tomatoes. Bring to the boil, reduce the heat and cover. Simmer gently for 25 minutes or until the potatoes are breaking up.

5 Stir in the parsley and pepper and add the reserved mussels in their shells. Heat through for 1 minute. Serve hot with a spoonful of yogurt.

Roasted Tomato and Pasta Soup

V

When the only tomatoes you can buy are not particularly flavoursome, make this soup. The roasting compensates for any lack of flavour in the tomatoes, and the soup has a wonderful, smoky taste.

INGREDIENTS

Serves 4

450g/1lb ripe Italian plum tomatoes, halved lengthways

1 large red (bell) pepper, quartered lengthways and seeded

1 large red onion, quartered lengthways

2 garlic cloves, unpeeled

15ml/1 tbsp olive oil

1.2 litres/2 pints/5 cups vegetable stock or water

a good pinch of granulated sugar

90g/3½ oz/scant 1 cup small pasta shapes, such as tubetti or small macaroni

salt and freshly ground black pepper

fresh basil leaves, to garnish

1 Preheat the oven to 190°C/ 375°F/Gas 5. Spread out the tomatoes, red pepper, onion and garlic in a roasting pan and drizzle with the olive oil. Roast for 30–40 minutes until the vegetables are soft and charred, stirring and turning them halfway through cooking.

2 Tip the vegetables into a food processor, add about 250ml/ 8fl oz/1 cup of the stock or water, and process until puréed. Scrape into a sieve placed over a large pan and press the purée through into the pan.

3 Add the remaining stock or water, the sugar and salt and pepper to taste. Bring to the boil.

4 Add the pasta and simmer for 7–8 minutes (or according to the instructions on the packet), stirring frequently, until *al dente*. Taste and adjust the seasoning with salt and freshly ground black pepper. Serve hot in warmed bowls, garnished with the fresh basil leaves.

> ### COOK'S TIP
> ~
> You can roast the vegetables in advance, allow them to cool, then leave them in a covered bowl in the refrigerator overnight before puréeing.

Sweetcorn and Scallop Chowder

Fresh sweetcorn is ideal for this chowder, although canned or frozen sweetcorn also works well. This soup is almost a meal in itself and makes a perfect lunch dish.

INGREDIENTS

Serves 4–6

2 sweetcorn cobs or 200g/7oz/generous
    1 cup frozen or canned sweetcorn
600ml/1 pint/2½ cups milk
15g/½ oz butter or margarine
1 small leek or onion, chopped
40g/1½ oz/¼ cup smoked streaky (fatty)
    bacon, finely chopped
1 small garlic clove, crushed
1 small green (bell) pepper, seeded
    and diced
1 celery stick, chopped
1 medium potato, diced
15ml/1 tbsp plain (all-purpose) flour
300ml/½ pint/1¼ cups chicken or
    vegetable stock
4 scallops
115g/4oz cooked fresh mussels
a pinch of paprika
150ml/¼ pint/⅔ cup single (light) cream
salt and freshly ground black pepper

1 Using a sharp knife, slice down the corn cobs to remove the kernels. Place half the kernels in a food processor or blender and process with a little of the milk. Set the other half aside.

2 Melt the butter or margarine in a large pan and gently fry the leek or onion, bacon and garlic over a low heat for 5 minutes until the leek is soft but not browned. Add the green pepper, celery and potato and sweat over a gentle heat for a further 3–4 minutes, stirring frequently.

3 Stir in the flour and cook for about 2 minutes until golden and frothy. Stir in a little milk and the corn mixture, the stock, the remaining milk and corn kernels and seasoning.

4 Bring to the boil, and then simmer, partially covered, for 15–20 minutes until the vegetables are tender.

5 Pull the corals away from the scallops and slice the white flesh into 5mm/¼in slices. Stir the scallops into the soup, cook for 4 minutes and then stir in the corals, mussels and paprika. Heat through for a few minutes and then stir in the cream. Check the seasoning and serve.

Clam Chowder

A traditional chowder from New England in the United States of America, the mixture of clams and pork, with potatoes and cream, is rich and utterly delicious.

INGREDIENTS

Serves 8

48 clams, scrubbed

1.5 litres/2½ pints/6¼ cups water

40g/1½ oz/¼ cup finely diced salt pork
   or bacon

3 medium onions, finely chopped

1 bay leaf

3 medium potatoes, diced

475ml/16fl oz/2 cups milk, warmed

250ml/8fl oz/1 cup single (light) cream

salt and freshly ground black pepper

chopped fresh parsley, to garnish

1 Rinse the clams well in cold water. Drain. Place them in a deep pan with the water and bring to the boil. Cover and steam for about 10 minutes until the shells open. Remove from the heat.

2 When the clams have cooled slightly, remove them from their shells. Discard any clams that have not opened. Chop the clams coarsely. Strain the cooking liquid through a sieve lined with muslin (cheesecloth) and reserve.

3 In a large, heavy pan, fry the salt pork or bacon until it renders its fat and begins to brown. Add the onions and cook over a low heat for 8–10 minutes until softened.

4 Stir in the bay leaf, potatoes, and clam cooking liquid. Bring to the boil and cook for 5–10 minutes.

5 Stir in the chopped clams. Continue to cook until the potatoes are tender, stirring from time to time. Season.

6 Stir in the warmed milk and cream and heat very gently for a further 5 minutes. Discard the bay leaf, adjust the seasoning and serve sprinkled with chopped fresh parsley.

Pork and Noodle Broth with Prawns

This delicately flavoured soup from Vietnam is quick and easy to make, while tasting really special. The noodles make the soup into a satisfying and wholesome dish.

INGREDIENTS

Serves 4–6

350g/12oz pork chops or
    fillet (tenderloin)
225g/8oz raw prawn (shrimp) tails or
    cooked prawns (shrimp)
150g/5oz thin egg noodles
15ml/1 tbsp vegetable oil
10ml/2 tsp sesame oil
4 shallots or 1 medium onion, sliced
15ml/1 tbsp finely sliced fresh root ginger
1 garlic clove, crushed
5ml/l tsp sugar
1.5 litres/2½ pints/6¼ cups
    chicken stock
2 kaffir lime leaves
45ml/3 tbsp fish sauce
juice of ½ lime

For the garnish
4 sprigs of fresh coriander (cilantro)
2 spring onions (scallions), green parts
    only, chopped

VARIATION
∾

This quick recipe can be made with 200g/7oz boneless chicken breast portions instead of pork fillet (tenderloin).

1 If you are using pork chops rather than fillet, remove any fat and the bones. Place the pork in the freezer for 30 minutes to firm, but not freeze it. The cold makes the meat easier to slice thinly. Once sliced, set aside.

2 If using raw prawn tails, peel and devein the prawns.

3 Bring a large pan of salted water to the boil and simmer the egg noodles according to the instructions on the packet. Drain and refresh under cold running water. Set the noodles to one side.

4 Preheat a wok. Add the vegetable and sesame oils and heat through. When the oil is hot, add the shallots or onion and stir-fry for 3–4 minutes, until evenly browned. Remove from the wok and set aside.

5 Add the ginger, garlic, sugar and chicken stock to the wok and bring to a simmer. Add the lime leaves, fish sauce and lime juice. Add the pork, then simmer for 15 minutes.

6 Add the prawns and noodles and simmer for 3–4 minutes, or longer if using raw prawns to ensure that they are cooked.

7 Serve garnished with coriander sprigs and the green parts of the spring onion.

Split Pea and Ham Soup

The main ingredient for this dish is bacon hock, which is the narrow piece of bone cut from a foreleg. You could use a piece of pork belly instead, if you prefer, and remove it with the herbs before serving.

INGREDIENTS

Serves 4

450g/1lb/2½ cups green split peas

4 rindless bacon rashers (strips)

1 onion, roughly chopped

2 carrots, sliced

1 celery stick, sliced

2.4 litres/4¼ pints/10½ cups cold water

1 sprig of fresh thyme

2 bay leaves

1 large potato, roughly diced

1 bacon hock

freshly ground black pepper

1 Put the split peas into a bowl, cover with cold water and leave to soak overnight.

2 Cut the bacon into small pieces. In a large pan, dry fry the bacon for 4–5 minutes or until crisp. Remove from the pan with a slotted spoon.

3 Add the chopped onion, carrots and celery to the fat in the pan and cook for 3–4 minutes until the onion is softened but not brown. Return the bacon to the pan with the water.

4 Drain the split peas and add to the pan with the thyme, bay leaves, potato and bacon. Bring to the boil, reduce the heat, cover and cook gently for 1 hour.

5 Remove the thyme, bay leaves and hock. Process the soup in a blender or food processor until smooth. Return to a clean pan. Cut the meat from the hock and add to the soup and heat through gently. Season with plenty of freshly ground black pepper. Ladle into warm soup bowls and serve.

Fish Ball Soup

The Japanese name for this soup is Tsumire-jiru. Tsumire, *means, quite literally, sardine balls, and these are added to this delicious soup to impart their robust flavour.*

INGREDIENTS

Serves 4

100ml/3¹⁄₂ fl oz/generous ¹⁄₃ cup sake or
   dry white wine
1.2 litres/2 pints/5 cups instant dashi
60ml/4 tbsp white miso paste
150g/5oz shimeji mushrooms or
   6 shiitake mushrooms
1 leek or large spring onion (scallion)

For the fish balls
20g/³⁄₄ oz fresh root ginger
800g/1³⁄₄ lb fresh sardines, gutted and
   heads removed
30ml/2 tbsp white miso paste
15ml/1 tbsp sake or dry white wine
7.5ml/1¹⁄₂ tsp sugar
1 egg
30ml/2 tbsp cornflour (cornstarch)

1 First make the fish balls. To do this, grate the ginger and squeeze it well to yield 5ml/1 tsp ginger juice.

2 Rinse the sardines under cold running water, then cut in half along the backbone. Remove all the bones. To skin a boned sardine, lay it skin side down on a board, then run a sharp knife slowly along the skin from tail to head.

3 Coarsely chop the sardines and process with the ginger juice, miso, sake or wine, sugar and egg to a thick paste in a food processor or blender. Transfer to a bowl and mix in the cornflour until thoroughly blended.

4 Trim the shimeji mushrooms and either separate each stem or remove the stems from the shiitake mushrooms and shred them. Cut the leek or spring onion into 4cm/1¹⁄₂in strips.

5 Bring the ingredients for the soup to the boil. Use two wet spoons to shape small portions of the sardine mixture into bitesize balls and drop them into the soup. Add the prepared mushrooms and leek or spring onion.

6 Simmer the soup until the sardine balls float to the surface. Serve immediately, in individual, deep soup bowls.

Three-delicacy Soup

This delicious soup combines the three ingredients of chicken, ham and prawns.

Serves 4

115g/4oz chicken breast fillet

115g/4oz honey-roast ham

115g/4oz peeled prawns (shrimp)

700ml/1¼ pints/3 cups chicken stock

salt

chopped spring onions (scallions),
    to garnish

1 Thinly slice the chicken and ham into small pieces. If the prawns are large, cut them in half lengthways.

2 In a wok or pan, bring the stock to a rolling boil and add the chicken, ham and prawns. Bring back to the boil, add salt to taste and simmer for 1 minute.

3 Ladle into individual soup bowls. Serve hot, garnished with chopped spring onions.

COOK'S TIP

Fresh, uncooked prawns (shrimp) impart the best flavour. If these are not available, you can use ready-cooked prawns. They must be added towards the end of cooking, to prevent over-cooking.

Lamb and Cucumber Soup

This is a very simple soup to prepare, but tastes delicious nevertheless.

Serves 4

225g/8oz lamb steak

15ml/1 tbsp light soy sauce

10ml/2 tsp Chinese rice wine or
    dry sherry

2.5ml/½ tsp sesame oil

7.5cm/3in piece cucumber

750ml/1¼ pints/3 cups chicken or
    vegetable stock

15ml/1 tbsp rice vinegar

salt and freshly ground white pepper

1 Trim off any excess fat from the lamb. Thinly slice the lamb into small pieces. Marinate in the soy sauce, wine or sherry and sesame oil for 25–30 minutes. Discard the marinade.

2 Halve the cucumber piece lengthways (do not peel), then cut into thin slices diagonally.

3 In a wok or pan, bring the stock to a rolling boil, add the lamb and stir to separate.

4 Return to the boil, then add the cucumber slices, vinegar and seasoning. Bring back to the boil and serve immediately.

Bulgarian Sour Lamb Soup

This traditional sour soup uses lamb, although pork and poultry are popular alternatives.

INGREDIENTS

Serves 4–5

30ml/2 tbsp oil

450g/11b lean lamb, trimmed and cubed

1 onion, diced

30ml/2 tbsp plain (all-purpose) flour

15ml/l tbsp paprika

1 litre/1¾ pints/4 cups hot lamb stock

3 sprigs of fresh parsley

4 spring onions (scallions)

4 sprigs of fresh dill

25g/1oz/scant ¼ cup long grain rice

2 eggs, beaten

30–45ml/2–3 tbsp or more vinegar or
   lemon juice

salt and freshly ground black pepper

For the garnish

25g/1oz/2 tbsp butter, melted

5ml/1 tsp paprika

a little fresh parsley or lovage and dill

1 In a large pan heat the oil and fry the meat until brown. Add the onion and cook until it has softened. Sprinkle in the flour and paprika. Stir well, add the stock and cook for 10 minutes.

2 Tie the parsley, spring onions and dill together with string and add to the pan with the rice and seasoning. Bring to the boil, then simmer gently for about 30–40 minutes, or until the lamb is tender.

3 Remove the pan from the heat and stir in the eggs. Add the vinegar or lemon juice. Discard the tied herbs and season to taste.

4 For the garnish, melt the butter in a pan and add the paprika. Ladle the soup into warmed serving bowls. Garnish with the herbs and a little red paprika butter.

Lentil, Bacon and Frankfurter Soup

This is a wonderfully hearty German soup, but a lighter version can be made by omitting the frankfurters, if preferred.

INGREDIENTS

Serves 6

225g/8oz/1 cup brown lentils

15ml/1 tbsp sunflower oil

1 onion, finely chopped

1 leek, finely chopped

1 carrot, finely diced

2 celery sticks, chopped

115g/4oz piece lean bacon

2 bay leaves

1.5 litres/2½ pints/6¼ cups water

30ml/2 tbsp chopped fresh parsley, plus extra to garnish

225g/8oz frankfurters, sliced

salt and freshly ground black pepper

1 Rinse the lentils thoroughly under cold running water, then drain.

2 Heat the oil in a large pan and gently fry the onion for 5 minutes until soft. Add the leek, carrot, celery, bacon and bay leaves.

COOK'S TIP
~

Unlike most pulses, brown lentils do not need to be soaked before cooking.

3 Add the lentils. Pour in the water, then slowly bring to the boil. Skim the surface, then simmer, half-covered, for about 45–50 minutes, or until the lentils are soft.

4 Remove the piece of bacon from the soup and cut into small cubes. Trim off any fat.

5 Return the bacon to the soup with the parsley and sliced frankfurters, and season well with salt and freshly ground black pepper. Simmer for 2–3 minutes, then remove the bay leaves.

6 Transfer to individual soup bowls and serve garnished with chopped parsley.

Chicken Minestrone

This is a special minestrone made with fresh chicken. Served with crusty bread, it is a meal in itself.

INGREDIENTS

Serves 4–6

15ml/1 tbsp olive oil

2 chicken thighs

3 rindless streaky (fatty) bacon rashers (strips), chopped

1 onion, finely chopped

a few fresh basil leaves, shredded

a few fresh rosemary leaves, finely chopped

15ml/1 tbsp chopped fresh flat leaf parsley

2 potatoes, cut into 1cm/½in cubes

1 large carrot, cut into 1cm/½in cubes

2 small courgettes (zucchini), cut into 1cm/½in cubes

1–2 celery sticks, cut into 1cm/½in cubes

1 litre/1¾ pints/4 cups chicken stock

200g/7oz/1¾ cups frozen peas

90g/3½oz/scant 1 cup stellette or other small soup pasta

salt and freshly ground black pepper

Parmesan cheese shavings, to serve

1 Heat the oil in a large frying pan, add the chicken thighs and fry for about 5 minutes on each side. Remove with a slotted spoon and set aside.

2 Add the bacon, onion and herbs to the pan and cook gently, stirring constantly, for 5 minutes. Add the potatoes, carrot, courgettes and celery and cook for 5 minutes more.

3 Return the chicken thighs to the pan, add the stock and bring to the boil. Cover and cook over a low heat for 35–40 minutes, stirring the soup occasionally.

4 Remove the chicken thighs with a slotted spoon and place them on a board. Stir the peas and pasta into the soup and bring back to the boil. Simmer, stirring frequently, for 7–8 minutes or according to the instructions on the packet, until the pasta is just *al dente*.

5 Meanwhile, remove and discard the chicken skin, then remove the meat from the chicken bones and cut it into small (1cm/½in) pieces.

6 Return the meat to the soup, stir well and heat through. Taste and adjust the seasoning as necessary.

7 Serve hot in warmed soup plates or bowls, topped with Parmesan shavings.

Meatball and Pasta Soup

This soup, which comes from sunny Sicily, is also substantial enough for a hearty supper, whatever the weather.

INGREDIENTS

Serves 4

2 x 300g/11oz cans condensed
    beef consommé
90g/3½oz/¾ cup very thin pasta, such as
    fidelini or spaghettini
chopped fresh flat leaf parsley, to garnish
grated Parmesan cheese, to serve

For the meatballs

1 very thick slice white bread, crusts
    removed
30ml/2 tbsp milk
225g/8oz/1 cup minced (ground) beef
1 garlic clove, crushed
30ml/2 tbsp grated Parmesan cheese
30–45ml/2–3 tbsp fresh flat leaf parsley
    leaves, coarsely chopped
1 egg
a generous pinch of freshly grated nutmeg
salt and freshly ground black pepper

1 Make the meatballs. Break the bread into a small bowl, add the milk and set aside to soak. Meanwhile, put the minced beef, garlic, Parmesan, parsley and egg in another large bowl. Grate the nutmeg liberally over the top and add salt and pepper to taste.

2 Squeeze the bread with your hands to remove as much milk as possible, then add the bread to the meatball mixture and mix everything together well with your hands. Wash your hands, rinse them under cold water, then form the mixture into tiny balls about the size of small marbles.

3 Tip both cans of consommé into a large pan, add water as directed on the labels, then add an extra can of water. Season to taste with salt and pepper, bring to the boil and add the meatballs.

4 Break the pasta into small pieces and add it to the soup. Bring to the boil, stirring gently. Simmer, stirring frequently, for 7–8 minutes or according to the instructions on the packet, until the pasta is *al dente*. Adjust the seasoning to taste.

5 Serve hot in warmed bowls, garnished with chopped parsley and freshly grated Parmesan cheese.

Tomato and Beef Soup

Fresh tomatoes and spring onions give this light beef broth a superb flavour.

INGREDIENTS

Serves 4

75g/3oz rump (round) steak, trimmed
900ml/1½ pints/3¾ cups beef stock
30ml/2 tbsp tomato purée (paste)
6 tomatoes, halved, seeded and chopped
10ml/2 tsp caster (superfine) sugar
15ml/1 tbsp cornflour (cornstarch)
15ml/1 tbsp cold water
1 egg white
2.5ml/½ tsp sesame oil
2 spring onions (scallions), shredded
salt and freshly ground black pepper

3 Mix the cornflour to a paste with the cold water. Add the paste to the soup, stirring constantly until it thickens slightly but does not become lumpy. Lightly beat the egg white in a cup.

4 Pour the egg white into the soup in a steady stream, stirring constantly. As soon as the egg white changes colour, add salt and pepper, stir the soup and pour it into heated bowls. Drizzle a few drops of sesame oil on each portion, sprinkle with the spring onions and serve.

1 Cut the beef into thin strips and place it in a pan. Pour over boiling water to cover. Cook for 2 minutes, then drain thoroughly and set aside.

2 Bring the stock to the boil in a clean pan. Stir in the tomato purée, then the tomatoes and sugar. Add the beef, allow the stock to boil again, then lower the heat and simmer for about 2 minutes.

Beef Broth with Cassava

This "big" soup is almost like a stew. The addition of wine is not traditional, but enhances the richness of the broth.

INGREDIENTS

Serves 4

450g/1lb stewing beef, cubed

1.2 litres/2 pints/5 cups beef stock

300ml/½ pint/1¼ cups white wine

15ml/1 tbsp soft brown sugar

1 onion, finely chopped

1 bay leaf

1 bouquet garni

1 sprig of fresh thyme

15ml/1 tbsp tomato purée (paste)

1 large carrot, sliced

275g/10oz cassava or yam, cubed

50g/2oz spinach, chopped

a little hot pepper sauce, to taste

salt and freshly ground black pepper

2 Add the carrot, cassava or yam, spinach, a few drops of hot pepper sauce, salt and pepper, and simmer for a further 15 minutes until both the meat and vegetables are tender. Serve.

1 Put the beef, stock, wine, sugar, onion, bay leaf, bouquet garni, thyme and tomato purée in a large pan, bring to the boil and then cover and simmer for about 1¼ hours.

COOK'S TIP

If you like, a cheap cut of lamb can be used instead of beef, and any other root vegetable can be used instead of, or as well as, the cassava or yam. Noodles, pasta shapes or macaroni can also be used as a base, in which case you can cut down on the root vegetables. You can, if you prefer, omit the wine and add more water.

ONE-POT-MEAL
SOUPS

V

Tuscan Bean Soup

There are many versions of this wonderful soup. This one uses cannellini beans, leeks, cabbage and good olive oil – and tastes even better when it is reheated.

INGREDIENTS

Serves 4

45ml/3 tbsp extra virgin olive oil
1 onion, roughly chopped
2 leeks, roughly chopped
1 large potato, diced
2 garlic cloves, finely chopped
1.2 litres/2 pints/5 cups vegetable stock
400g/14oz can cannellini beans, drained
   and liquid reserved
175g/6oz Savoy cabbage, shredded
45ml/3 tbsp chopped fresh flat leaf parsley
30ml/2 tbsp chopped fresh oregano
75g/3oz Parmesan cheese, shaved
salt and freshly ground black pepper

For the garlic toasts

30–45ml/2–3 tbsp extra virgin olive oil
6 thick slices rustic bread
1 garlic clove, peeled and bruised

1 Heat the oil in a large pan and gently cook the onion, leeks, potato and garlic for 4–5 minutes until they are just beginning to soften.

2 Pour on the stock and the liquid from the beans. Cover and simmer for 15 minutes.

3 Stir in the cabbage, beans and half the herbs, season and cook for a further 10 minutes. Spoon about one-third of the soup into a food processor or blender and process until fairly smooth. Return to the soup in the pan, adjust the seasoning and heat through for 5 minutes.

4 Make the garlic toasts. Drizzle a little oil over the slices of bread, then rub both sides of each slice with the garlic. Toast until browned on both sides. Ladle the soup into bowls. Sprinkle with the remaining herbs and the Parmesan shavings. Add a drizzle of olive oil and serve with the hot garlic toasts.

Farmhouse Soup

Root vegetables form the base of this chunky, minestrone-style, main-meal soup. You can vary the vegetables according to what you have to hand.

INGREDIENTS

Serves 4

30ml/2 tbsp olive oil

1 onion, roughly chopped

3 carrots, cut into large chunks

175–200g/6–7oz turnips, cut into
    large chunks

about 175g/6oz swede (rutabaga), cut into
    large chunks

400g/14oz can chopped Italian tomatoes

15ml/1 tbsp tomato purée (paste)

5ml/1 tsp dried mixed herbs

5ml/1 tsp dried oregano

50g/2oz/½ cup dried (bell) peppers,
    thinly sliced (optional)

1.5 litres/2½ pints/6¼ cups vegetable
    stock or water

50g/2oz/½ cup small macaroni
    or conchiglie

400g/14oz can red kidney beans, rinsed
    and drained

30ml/2 tbsp chopped fresh flat leaf parsley

salt and freshly ground black pepper

grated Parmesan cheese, to serve

1 Heat the oil in a large pan, add the onion and cook over a low heat for about 5 minutes until softened. Add the fresh vegetables, canned tomatoes, tomato purée, dried herbs and dried peppers, if using. Season with salt and pepper to taste.

2 Pour in the stock or water and bring to the boil. Stir well, cover, lower the heat and simmer gently for 30 minutes, stirring occasionally.

3 Add the pasta and bring to the boil, stirring. Lower the heat and simmer, uncovered, for about 5 minutes or according to the instructions on the packet until the pasta is just *al dente*. Stir frequently during the cooking.

4 Stir in the beans. Heat through for 2–3 minutes, then remove from the heat and stir in the parsley. Taste and adjust the seasoning. Serve hot in warmed soup bowls and hand around the grated Parmesan separately.

COOK'S TIP

Packets of dried Italian (bell) peppers are sold in supermarkets and in delicatessens. They are piquant and firm with a "meaty" bite to them, which makes them ideal for adding substance to vegetarian soups.

Provençal Vegetable Soup

V

This satisfying soup captures all the flavours of summer in Provence. The basil and garlic purée, pistou, gives it extra colour and a wonderful aroma – so don't leave it out.

INGREDIENTS

Serves 6–8

275g/10oz/1½ cups shelled fresh broad
    (fava) beans or 175g/6oz/¾ cup dried
    haricot (navy) beans, soaked overnight
2.5ml/½ tsp dried herbes de Provence
2 garlic cloves, finely chopped
15ml/1 tbsp olive oil
1 onion, finely chopped
1 large leek, thinly sliced
1 celery stick, thinly sliced
2 carrots, finely diced
2 small potatoes, finely diced
115g/4oz green beans
1.2 litres/2 pints/5 cups water
2 small courgettes (zucchini),
    finely chopped
3 medium tomatoes, peeled, seeded and
    finely chopped
115g/4oz/l cup shelled garden peas, fresh
    or frozen
a handful of spinach leaves, cut into
    thin ribbons
salt and freshly ground black pepper
sprigs of fresh basil, to garnish

For the pistou
1 or 2 garlic cloves, finely chopped
15g/½ oz/½ cup fresh basil leaves
60ml/4 tbsp grated Parmesan cheese
60ml/4 tbsp extra virgin olive oil

1 To make the pistou, put the garlic, basil and Parmesan cheese in a food processor and process until smooth, scraping down the sides once. With the machine running, slowly add the olive oil through the feed tube. Alternatively, pound the garlic, basil and cheese in a mortar with a pestle and stir in the oil.

2 To make the soup, if using dried haricot beans, drain them, place in a pan and cover with water. Boil vigorously for 10 minutes and drain.

3 Place the par-boiled beans, or fresh beans if using, in a pan with the herbes de Provence and one of the garlic cloves. Add water to cover by 2.5cm/1in. Bring to the boil, reduce the heat and simmer over a medium-low heat until tender – about 10 minutes for fresh beans or 1 hour for dried beans. Set the beans aside in the cooking liquid.

4 Heat the oil in a large pan or flameproof casserole. Add the onion and leek and cook for about 5 minutes, stirring occasionally, until they begin to soften.

5 Add the celery, carrots and the remaining garlic clove and cook, covered, for 10 minutes, stirring occasionally.

6 Add the potatoes, green beans and water, then season lightly with salt and pepper. Bring to the boil, skimming any foam that rises to the surface, then reduce the heat, cover and simmer gently for 10 minutes.

7 Add the courgettes, tomatoes and peas, together with the reserved beans and their cooking liquid, and simmer for about 25–30 minutes until all the vegetables are tender. Add the spinach and simmer for 5 minutes. Season the soup and swirl a spoonful of pistou into each bowl. Garnish with basil and serve.

COOK'S TIP

Both the pistou and the soup can be made 2 days in advance and chilled. To serve, reheat gently, stirring occasionally.

Chunky Pasta Soup

V

Serve this hearty, main-meal soup with tasty, pesto-topped French bread croûtons.

Serves 4

115g/4oz/½ cup dried beans (a mixture of red kidney and haricot (navy) beans), soaked overnight

1.2 litres/2 pints/5 cups water

15ml/1 tbsp oil

1 onion, chopped

2 celery sticks, thinly sliced

2–3 garlic cloves, crushed

2 leeks, thinly sliced

1 vegetable stock (bouillon) cube

400g/14oz can or jar pimientos

45–60ml/3–4 tbsp tomato purée (paste)

115g/4oz pasta shapes

4 slices French bread

15ml/1 tbsp pesto sauce

115g/4oz/l cup baby corn, halved

50g/2oz each broccoli and cauliflower florets

a few drops of Tabasco sauce

salt and freshly ground black pepper

1 Drain the beans and place in a large pan with the water. Bring to the boil and simmer for about 1 hour, or until nearly tender.

2 When the beans are almost ready, heat the oil in a large pan and fry the vegetables for 2 minutes. Add the stock cube and the beans with about 600ml/ 1 pint/2½ cups of their liquid. Cover and simmer for 10 minutes.

3 Meanwhile, purée the pimientos with a little of their liquid and add to the pan. Stir in the tomato purée and pasta and cook for 15 minutes. Preheat the oven to 200°C/400°F/Gas 6.

4 Meanwhile, make the pesto croûtons. Spread the French bread with the pesto sauce and bake for 10 minutes or until crisp.

5 When the pasta is just cooked, add the baby corn, broccoli and cauliflower florets, Tabasco sauce and seasoning to taste. Heat through for 2–3 minutes and serve immediately with the croûtons.

Caribbean Vegetable Soup

V

*This vegetable soup is refreshing
and filling, and a good choice for
a main lunch dish.*

INGREDIENTS

Serves 4

25g/1oz/2 tbsp butter or margarine

1 onion, chopped

1 garlic clove, crushed

2 carrots, sliced

1.5 litres/2½ pints/6¼ cups vegetable
    stock

2 bay leaves

2 sprigs of fresh thyme

1 celery stick, finely chopped

2 green bananas, peeled and cut into
    four pieces

175g/6oz white yam or eddo, peeled
    and cubed

25g/1oz/2 tbsp red lentils

1 christophene (chayote), peeled
    and chopped

25g/1oz/2 tbsp macaroni (optional)

salt and freshly ground black pepper

chopped spring onions (scallions),
    to garnish

COOK'S TIP

Use other root vegetables or
potatoes if yam or eddoes are
not available. Add more stock if
you want a thinner soup.

1 Melt the butter or margarine
and fry the onion, garlic and
carrots for a few minutes, stirring
occasionally, until beginning to
soften. Add the stock, bay leaves
and thyme and bring to the boil.

2 Add the celery, green bananas,
white yam or eddo, lentils,
christophene and macaroni, if
using. Season and simmer for
25 minutes or until all the vegetables
are cooked. Serve garnished with
chopped spring onions.

Bouillabaisse

Perhaps the most famous of all Mediterranean fish soups, this recipe, originating from Marseilles in the south of France, is a rich and colourful mixture of fish and shellfish, flavoured with tomatoes, saffron and orange.

INGREDIENTS

Serves 4–6

1.5kg/3–3½ lb mixed fish and raw
    shellfish, such as red mullet, John Dory,
    monkfish, red snapper, whiting, large
    raw prawns (shrimp) and clams
225g/8oz well-flavoured tomatoes
a pinch of saffron threads
90ml/6 tbsp olive oil
1 onion, sliced
1 leek, sliced
1 celery stick, sliced
2 garlic cloves, crushed
1 bouquet garni
1 strip of orange rind
2.5ml/½ tsp fennel seeds
15ml/1 tbsp tomato purée (paste)
10ml/2 tsp Pernod
salt and freshly ground black pepper
4–6 thick slices French bread and
    45ml/3 tbsp chopped fresh parsley,
    to serve

COOK'S TIP

Saffron comes from the orange and red stigmas of a type of crocus, which must be harvested by hand and is therefore extremely expensive – the highest-priced spice in the world. However, its flavour is unique and cannot be replaced by any other spice. It is an essential ingredient in traditional bouillabaisse and should not be omitted.

1 Remove the heads, tails and fins from the fish and set the fish aside. Put the trimmings in a large pan with 1.2 litres/2 pints/ 5 cups water. Bring to the boil and simmer for 15 minutes. Strain and reserve the liquid.

2 Cut the fish into large chunks. Leave the shellfish in their shells. Scald the tomatoes, then drain and refresh in cold water. Peel them and chop roughly. Soak the saffron in 15–30ml/1–2 tbsp hot water.

3 Heat the oil in a large pan, add the onion, leek and celery and cook until softened. Add the garlic, bouquet garni, orange rind, fennel seeds and chopped tomatoes, then stir in the saffron and its soaking liquid and the reserved fish stock. Season with salt and pepper, then bring to the boil and simmer for 30–40 minutes.

4 Add the shellfish and boil for about 6 minutes. Add the fish and cook for 6–8 minutes more, until it flakes easily.

5 Using a slotted spoon, transfer the fish to a warmed serving platter. Keep the liquid boiling, to allow the oil to emulsify with the broth. Add the tomato purée and Pernod, then check the seasoning.

6 Ladle into warm bowls, scatter with chopped parsley and serve with French bread.

Prawn Creole

Prawns are combined with chopped fresh vegetables and cayenne pepper to make this tasty soup.

INGREDIENTS

Serves 4

675g/1½lb raw prawns (shrimp) in the
    shell, with heads, if available
475ml/16fl oz/2 cups water
45ml/3 tbsp olive or vegetable oil
175g/6oz/1½ cups very finely
    chopped onions
75g/3oz/½ cup celery, very finely chopped
75g/3oz/½ cup green (bell) pepper, very
    finely chopped
25g/1oz/½ cup fresh parsley, chopped
1 garlic clove, crushed
15ml/1 tbsp Worcestershire sauce
1.5ml/¼ tsp cayenne pepper
120ml/4fl oz/½ cup dry white wine
50g/2oz/1 cup plum tomatoes, peeled
    and chopped
5ml/1 tsp salt
1 bay leaf
5ml/1 tsp sugar
fresh parsley, to garnish
boiled rice, to serve

1 Peel and devein the prawns, reserving the heads and shells. Set the prawns aside in a covered bowl in the refrigerator.

2 Put the prawn heads and shells in a pan with the water. Bring to the boil and simmer for 15 minutes. Strain and reserve 350ml/12fl oz/1½ cups of the prawn stock.

3 Heat the oil in a heavy pan. Add the onions and cook over a low heat for 8–10 minutes until softened. Add the celery and green pepper and cook for 5 minutes further. Stir in the parsley, garlic, Worcestershire sauce and cayenne. Cook for another 5 minutes.

4 Raise the heat to medium. Stir in the wine and simmer for 3–4 minutes. Add the tomatoes, reserved prawn stock, salt, bay leaf and sugar and bring to the boil. Stir well, then reduce the heat to low and simmer for about 30 minutes until the tomatoes have fallen apart and the sauce has reduced slightly. Remove from the heat and cool slightly.

5 Discard the bay leaf. Pour the sauce into a food processor or blender and process until quite smooth. Taste and adjust the seasoning as necessary.

6 Return the tomato sauce to the pan and bring to the boil. Add the prawns and simmer for 4–5 minutes until they turn pink. Ladle into individual soup bowls, garnish with fresh parsley and serve with rice.

Clam and Pasta Soup

This soup is a variation of spaghetti alle vongole. Serve it with hot focaccia or ciabatta bread for an informal supper with friends.

Serves 4

30ml/2 tbsp olive oil

1 large onion, finely chopped

2 garlic cloves, crushed

400g/14oz can chopped tomatoes

15ml/1 tbsp sun-dried tomato purée (paste)

5ml/1 tsp granulated sugar

5ml/1 tsp dried mixed herbs

about 750ml/1¼ pints/3 cups fish or vegetable stock

150ml/¼ pint/⅔ cup red wine

50g/2oz/½ cup small pasta shapes

150g/5oz jar or can clams in natural juice

30ml/2 tbsp finely chopped fresh flat leaf parsley, plus a few whole leaves to garnish

salt and freshly ground black pepper

1 Heat the oil in a large pan. Cook the onion gently for about 5 minutes, stirring frequently, until softened.

2 Add the garlic, tomatoes, tomato purée, sugar, herbs, stock and wine, with salt and pepper to taste. Bring to the boil. Lower the heat, half-cover the pan and simmer for 10 minutes, stirring occasionally.

3 Add the pasta and continue simmering, uncovered, for about 10 minutes or until *al dente*. Stir occasionally to prevent the pasta from sticking together.

4 Add the clams and their juice to the soup and heat through for 4 minutes, adding more stock if required. Do not allow it to boil, or the clams will become tough. Remove from the heat, stir in the chopped parsley and adjust the seasoning. Serve hot, sprinkled with coarsely ground black pepper and parsley leaves.

Sweetcorn Chowder with Conchigliette

Sweetcorn kernels combine with smoked turkey and pasta to make this satisfying and filling one-pot meal, perfect for a hungry family.

INGREDIENTS

Serves 6–8

1 small green (bell) pepper

450g/1lb potatoes, diced

350g/12oz/2 cups canned or frozen
    sweetcorn kernels

1 onion, chopped

1 celery stick, chopped

1 bouquet garni

600ml/1 pint/2½ cups chicken stock

300ml/½ pint/1¼ cups skimmed milk

50g/2oz conchigliette

oil, for frying

150g/5oz smoked turkey rashers
    (strips), diced

salt and freshly ground black pepper

bread sticks, to serve

3 Add the milk and salt and pepper. Process half of the soup in a food processor or blender and return to the pan with the pasta. Simmer for 10 minutes or until the pasta is *al dente*.

4 Heat the oil in a non-stick frying pan and fry the turkey rashers quickly for 2–3 minutes. Stir into the soup. Serve the soup with bread sticks.

1 Seed the green pepper and cut into dice. Cover with boiling water and leave to stand for 2 minutes. Drain and rinse.

2 Put the potatoes into a pan with the sweetcorn, onion, celery, diced pepper, bouquet garni and stock. Bring to the boil, cover and simmer for 20 minutes until tender.

Japanese Crushed Tofu Soup

V

The main ingredient for this soup is crushed tofu, which is both nutritious and satisfying.

INGREDIENTS

Serves 4

150g/5oz fresh tofu, weighed
   without water

2 dried shiitake mushrooms

50g/2oz gobo

5ml/1 tsp rice vinegar

1/2 black or white konnyaku
   (about 115g/4oz)

30ml/2 tbsp sesame oil

115g/4oz mooli (daikon), thinly sliced

50g/2oz carrot, thinly sliced

750ml/1¼ pints/3 cups kombu and
   bonito stock or instant dashi

a pinch of salt

30ml/2 tbsp sake or dry white wine

7.5ml/1½ tsp mirin

45ml/3 tbsp white or red miso paste

a dash of soy sauce

6 mangetouts (snow peas), trimmed,
   boiled and thinly sliced, to garnish

1 Crush the tofu roughly by hand until it resembles lumpy scrambled egg in texture – do not crush it too finely.

2 Wrap the tofu in a clean dishtowel and put it in a sieve, then pour over plenty of boiling water. Leave the tofu to drain thoroughly for 10 minutes.

3 Soak the dried shiitake mushrooms in tepid water for 20 minutes, then drain them. Remove their stems and cut the caps into four to six pieces.

4 Use a vegetable brush to scrub the skin off the gobo and slice it into thin shavings. Soak the shavings for 5 minutes in cold water with the vinegar added to remove any bitter taste. Drain.

5 Put the konnyaku in a small pan and cover with water. Bring to the boil, then drain and cool. Tear the konnyaku into 2cm/3/4in lumps: do not use a knife, as smooth cuts will prevent it from absorbing flavour.

6 Heat the sesame oil in a deep pan. Add all the shiitake mushrooms, gobo, mooli, carrot and konnyaku. Stir-fry for 1 minute, add the tofu and stir well.

7 Pour in the stock/dashi and add the salt, sake or wine and mirin. Bring to the boil. Skim the broth and simmer it for 5 minutes.

8 In a small bowl, dissolve the miso paste in a little of the soup, then return it to the pan. Simmer the soup gently for 10 minutes, until the vegetables are soft. Add the soy sauce, then remove from the heat. Serve immediately in four bowls, garnished with the mangetouts.

Fisherman's Soup

There is something truly delicious about the combined flavours of bacon and fish.

Serves 4

6 streaky (fatty) bacon rashers (strips), cut into thin strips

15g/½ oz/1 tbsp butter

1 large onion, chopped

1 garlic clove, finely chopped

30ml/2 tbsp chopped fresh parsley

5ml/1 tsp fresh thyme leaves

450g/1lb tomatoes, peeled, seeded and chopped

150ml/¼ pint/⅔ cup dry vermouth or white wine

450ml/¾ pint/scant 2 cups fish stock

300g/11oz potatoes, diced

675–900g/1½–2lb skinless white fish fillets, cut into large chunks

salt and freshly ground black pepper

fresh flat leaf parsley, to garnish

1 Fry the bacon in a large pan over moderate heat until lightly browned but not crisp. Remove from the pan and drain on kitchen paper.

2 Add the butter to the pan and cook the onion, stirring occasionally, for 3–5 minutes until soft. Add the garlic and herbs and continue cooking for 1 minute, stirring. Add the tomatoes, vermouth or wine and stock and bring to the boil.

3 Reduce the heat, cover and simmer the soup for 15 minutes. Add the potatoes, cover again and simmer for a further 10–12 minutes or until the potatoes are almost tender.

COOK'S TIP

In winter, when fresh tomatoes are lacking in flavour, you can substitute canned chopped tomatoes. The soup will taste slightly different but will still be successful.

4 Add the chunks of fish and the bacon strips. Simmer gently, uncovered, for 5 minutes or until the fish is just cooked and the potatoes are tender. Adjust the seasoning, garnish with flat leaf parsley and serve.

Chunky Chicken Soup

This thick chicken and vegetable soup is served with garlic-flavoured fried croûtons.

INGREDIENTS

Serves 4

4 skinless, boneless chicken thighs

15g/½oz/1 tbsp butter

2 small leeks, thinly sliced

25g/1oz/2 tbsp long grain rice

900ml/1½ pints/3¾ cups chicken stock

15ml/1 tbsp chopped mixed fresh parsley and mint

salt and freshly ground black pepper

For the garlic croûtons

30ml/2 tbsp olive oil

1 garlic clove, crushed

4 slices bread, cut into cubes

1 Cut the chicken into 1cm/½in cubes. Melt the butter in a pan, add the leeks and cook until tender. Add the rice and chicken and cook for 2 minutes.

2 Add the stock, then cover the pan and simmer gently for 15–20 minutes until tender.

3 To make the garlic croûtons, heat the oil in a large frying pan. Add the crushed garlic clove and bread cubes and cook until the bread is golden brown, stirring constantly to prevent burning. Drain on kitchen paper and sprinkle with a pinch of salt.

4 Add the parsley and mint to the soup and adjust the seasoning to taste. Serve with the garlic croûtons.

Noodles in Soup

In China, noodles in soup are far more popular than fried noodles, as in Europe. You can adapt this basic recipe by using different "dressing" ingredients .

Serves 4

225g/8oz chicken breast fillet, pork fillet (tenderloin) or ready-cooked meat

3–4 shiitake mushrooms, soaked

115g/4oz canned sliced bamboo shoots, drained

115g/4oz spinach leaves, lettuce hearts, or Chinese leaves (Chinese cabbage)

2 spring onions (scallions)

350g/12oz dried egg noodles

600ml/1 pint/2½ cups stock

30ml/2 tbsp vegetable oil

5ml/1 tsp salt

2.5ml/½ tsp light brown sugar

15ml/1 tbsp light soy sauce

10ml/2 tsp Chinese rice wine or dry sherry

a few drops of sesame oil

red chilli sauce, to serve

1 Thinly shred the meat. Squeeze dry the shiitake mushrooms and discard any hard stalks. Then thinly shred the mushrooms, bamboo shoots, greens and spring onions.

2 Cook the noodles in boiling water according to the instructions on the packet, then drain and rinse under cold water. Place in a serving bowl.

3 Bring the stock to the boil and pour over the noodles. Set aside and keep warm.

4 Heat the oil in a preheated wok, add about half of the spring onions and the meat, and stir-fry for about 1 minute.

5 Add the mushrooms, bamboo shoots and greens and stir-fry for 1 minute. Add the salt, sugar, soy sauce and rice wine or sherry and blend well.

6 Pour the "dressing" over the noodles, garnish with the remaining spring onions, sprinkle over a few drops of sesame oil. Divide among individual soup bowls and serve immediately with hot red chilli sauce.

Chicken Soup with Vermicelli

In Morocco, the cook – who is almost always the most senior female of the household – would use a whole chicken for this nourishing soup, to serve to her large extended family. This is a slightly simplified version, using chicken portions.

INGREDIENTS

Serves 4–6

30ml/2 tbsp sunflower oil

15g/¹⁄₂oz/1 tbsp butter

1 onion, chopped

2 chicken legs or breast portions, halved
   or quartered

flour, for dusting

2 carrots, cut into 4cm/1¹⁄₂in pieces

1 parsnip, cut into 4cm/1¹⁄₂in pieces

1.5 litres/2¹⁄₂ pints/6¹⁄₄ cups chicken stock

1 cinnamon stick

a good pinch of paprika

a pinch of saffron

2 egg yolks

juice of ¹⁄₂ lemon

30ml/2 tbsp chopped fresh
   coriander (cilantro)

30ml/2 tbsp chopped fresh parsley

150g/5oz vermicelli

salt and freshly ground black pepper

1 Heat the oil and butter in a pan or flameproof casserole, and fry the onion for 3–4 minutes until softened. Dust the chicken pieces in seasoned flour and fry gently until evenly browned.

2 Transfer the chicken to a plate and add the carrots and parsnip to the pan. Cook over a gentle heat for 3–4 minutes, stirring frequently, then return the chicken to the pan. Add the stock, cinnamon stick and paprika and season well with salt and pepper.

3 Bring the soup to the boil, cover and simmer for 1 hour until the vegetables are very tender.

4 Meanwhile, blend the saffron in 30ml/2 tbsp boiling water. Beat the egg yolks with the lemon juice in a separate bowl and add the coriander and parsley. When the saffron water has cooled, stir into the egg and lemon mixture.

5 When the vegetables are tender, transfer the chicken to a plate. Spoon away any excess fat from the soup, then increase the heat a little and stir in the noodles. Cook for 6 minutes until the noodles are tender. Meanwhile, remove the skin and bones from the chicken and chop the flesh into bitesize pieces.

6 When the vermicelli is cooked stir in the chicken pieces and the egg, lemon and saffron mixture. Cook over a low heat for 2 minutes, stirring constantly. Adjust the seasoning and serve.

Noodle Soup with Pork and Sichuan Pickle

This soup is a meal in itself and the hot pickle gives it a delicious tang.

INGREDIENTS

Serves 4

1 litre/1¾ pints/4 cups chicken stock

350g/12oz egg noodles

15ml/1 tbsp dried prawns (shrimp), soaked in water

30ml/2 tbsp vegetable oil

225g/8oz lean pork, finely shredded

15ml/1 tbsp yellow bean paste

15ml/1 tbsp soy sauce

115g/4oz Sichuan hot pickle, rinsed, drained and shredded

a pinch of sugar

2 spring onions (scallions), thinly sliced, to garnish

1 Bring the stock to the boil in a large pan. Add the noodles and cook until almost tender. Drain the dried prawns, rinse them under cold water, drain again and add to the stock. Lower the heat and simmer for a further 2 minutes. Keep hot.

2 Heat the oil in a frying pan or wok. Add the pork and stir-fry over a high heat for 3 minutes.

3 Add the bean paste and soy sauce to the pork and stir-fry for 1 minute. Add the hot pickle with a pinch of sugar. Stir-fry for 1 minute further.

4 Divide the noodles and soup among individual serving bowls. Spoon the pork mixture on top, then sprinkle with the spring onions and serve immediately.

Cock-a-leekie

This traditional soup recipe originally included beef as well as chicken. In the olden days, it would have been made from an old cock bird, hence the name.

Serves 4

2 chicken portions, (about 275g/10oz each)

1.2 litres/2 pints/5 cups chicken stock

1 bouquet garni

4 leeks

8–12 prunes, soaked

salt and freshly ground black pepper

bread, to serve

1 Put the chicken portions into a pan with the stock and bouquet garni. Bring to the boil and simmer gently for 40 minutes.

2 Cut the white part of the leeks into 2.5cm/1in slices and finely slice a little of the green part.

3 Add the white part of the leeks and the prunes to the pan and cook gently for 20 minutes, then add the green part of the leeks and cook for a further 10–15 minutes.

4 Remove the bouquet garni and discard. Take the chicken out of the pan, discard the skin and bones, and chop the flesh. Return the chopped flesh to the pan and season the soup.

5 Heat the soup through gently. Ladle into warm soup bowls and serve hot with bread.

Scotch Broth

Sustaining and warming, Scotch Broth makes a delicious one-pot meal anywhere.

Serves 6

900g/2lb lean neck of lamb, cut into large, even-sized chunks

1.75 litres/3 pints/7½ cups water

1 large onion, chopped

50g/2oz/¼ cup pearl barley

1 bouquet garni

1 large carrot, chopped

1 turnip, chopped

3 leeks, chopped

½ small white cabbage, shredded

salt and freshly ground black pepper

chopped fresh parsley, to garnish (optional)

1 Put the lamb and water into a large pan and bring to the boil. Skim off any scum that rises to the surface, then stir in the onion, barley and bouquet garni.

2 Bring the soup back to the boil, partly cover the pan and simmer gently for 1 hour. Add the remaining vegetables and the seasoning, bring back to the boil, partly cover again and simmer gently for about 35 minutes until the vegetables are tender.

3 Remove any surplus fat from the top of the soup. Serve the soup hot, sprinkled with chopped parsley, if liked.

Smoked Turkey and Lentil Soup

Lentils seem to enhance the flavour of smoked turkey, and combined with four tasty vegetables, they make a fine meal-in-a-pot.

INGREDIENTS

Serves 4

25g/1oz/2 tbsp butter

1 large carrot, chopped

1 onion, chopped

1 leek, white part only, chopped

1 celery stick, chopped

115g/4oz/1½ cups mushrooms, chopped

50ml/2fl oz/¼ cup dry white wine

1.2 litres/2 pints/5 cups chicken stock

10ml/2 tsp dried thyme

1 bay leaf

115g/4oz/½ cup lentils

75g/3oz smoked turkey meat, diced

salt and freshly ground black pepper

1 Melt the butter in a large pan. Add the carrot, onion, leek, celery and mushrooms. Cook for 3–5 minutes until golden.

2 Stir in the wine and chicken stock. Bring to the boil and skim off any foam that rises to the surface. Add the thyme and bay leaf. Lower the heat, cover and simmer gently for 30 minutes.

3 Add the lentils and continue cooking, covered, for a further 30–40 minutes until they are just tender. Stir the soup occasionally.

4 Add the turkey and season to taste with salt and pepper. Cook until just heated through. Ladle into bowls and serve.

Spinach and Lemon Soup with Meatballs

This soup, known as aarshe saak, *is almost standard fare in many parts of the Middle East. In Greece, it is made without the meatballs and is called* avgolemono.

INGREDIENTS

Serves 6

2 large onions

45ml/3 tbsp oil

15ml/1 tbsp ground turmeric

115g/4oz/½ cup yellow split peas

1.2 litres/2 pints/5 cups water

225g/8oz minced (ground) lamb

450g/1lb spinach, chopped

50g/2oz/½ cup rice flour

juice of 2 lemons

1–2 garlic cloves, finely chopped

30ml/2 tbsp chopped fresh mint

4 eggs, beaten

salt and freshly ground black pepper

sprigs of fresh mint, to garnish

1 Chop one of the onions and fry in 30ml/2 tbsp of the oil in a large pan until golden. Add the turmeric, peas and water and bring to the boil. Simmer for 20 minutes.

2 Grate the other onion into a bowl, add the lamb and seasoning and mix well. Using your hands, form the mixture into small balls, about the size of walnuts. Carefully add to the pan and simmer for 10 minutes, then add the spinach, cover and simmer for 20 minutes.

3 Mix the flour with about 250ml/8fl oz/1 cup cold water to make a smooth paste, then gradually add to the pan, stirring constantly. Add the lemon juice, season and cook over a gentle heat for 20 minutes.

4 Meanwhile, heat the remaining oil in a small pan and fry the garlic briefly until golden. Stir in the mint and remove the pan from the heat.

5 Remove the soup from the heat and stir in the beaten eggs. Sprinkle the prepared garlic and mint mixture over the soup, garnish with mint sprigs and serve immediately.

Seafood and Sausage Gumbo

Gumbo is a soup, but is often served over rice as a main course.

Serves 10–12

1.5kg/3lb raw prawns (shrimp) in shells

1.5 litres/2½ pints/7 cups water

4 medium onions,

4 bay leaves

175ml/6fl oz/¾ cup vegetable oil

115g/4oz/1 cup flour

60ml/5 tbsp margarine or butter

2 green (bell) peppers, seeded and
    finely chopped

4 celery sticks, finely chopped

675g/1½ lb Polish or andouille sausage,
    cut into 1cm/½ in slices

450g/1lb fresh okra, cut into 1cm/
    ½ in slices

3 garlic cloves, crushed

2.5ml/½ tsp fresh or dried thyme leaves

10ml/2 tsp salt

2.5ml/½ tsp freshly ground black pepper

2.5ml/½ tsp white pepper

5ml/1 tsp cayenne pepper

475ml/16fl oz hot pepper sauce (optional)

250g/9oz/2 cups chopped, peeled, fresh or
    canned plum tomatoes

450g/1lb fresh crab meat

boiled rice, to serve

1 Peel and devein the prawns; reserve the heads and shells. Cover and chill the prawns while you make the sauce.

2 Place the prawn heads and shells in a pan with the water, quartered onion and one of the bay leaves. Bring to the boil, then partly cover and simmer for 20 minutes. Strain and set aside.

3 To make a Cajun roux, heat the oil in a heavy frying pan. When the oil is hot, add the flour, a little at a time, and blend to a smooth paste.

4 Cook over a medium-low heat, stirring constantly for 25–40 minutes until the roux reaches the colour of peanut butter. Remove the pan from the heat and continue stirring until the roux has cooled and stopped cooking.

5 Melt the margarine or butter in a large, heavy pan or flameproof casserole. Finely chop the remaining onions and add to the pan with the peppers and celery. Cook over a medium-low heat for about 8 minutes, until the onions are softened, stirring occasionally.

6 Add the sausage and mix well. Cook for 5 minutes more. Add the okra and garlic, stir, and cook until the okra stops producing white "threads".

7 Add the remaining bay leaves, the thyme, salt, black and white peppers, cayenne pepper, and hot pepper sauce to taste, if using. Mix well. Stir in 1.35 litres/ 2¼ pints/6 cups of the prawn stock and the tomatoes. Bring to the boil, partly cover the pan, lower the heat and simmer for about 20 minutes.

8 Whisk in the Cajun roux. Raise the heat and bring to the boil, whisking well. Lower the heat again and simmer, uncovered, for a further 40–45 minutes, stirring occasionally.

9 Gently stir in the prawns and crab meat. Cook for 3–4 minutes until the prawns turn pink.

10 To serve, put a mound of hot boiled rice in each serving bowl and ladle on the gumbo, making sure each person gets some prawns, some crab meat and some sausage.

Green Herb Gumbo

Traditionally served at the end of Lent, this is a joyful, sweetly spiced and revitalizing dish, even if you haven't been fasting. The variety of green ingredients is important, so buy substitutes if you cannot find all of them.

INGREDIENTS

Serves 6–8

350g/12oz piece raw smoked gammon (cured ham)

30ml/2 tbsp lard or cooking oil

1 large Spanish onion, roughly chopped

2–3 garlic cloves, crushed

5ml/1 tsp dried oregano

5ml/1 tsp dried thyme

2 bay leaves

2 cloves

2 celery sticks, thinly sliced

1 green (bell) pepper, seeded and chopped

½ medium green cabbage, stalked and finely shredded

2 litres/3½ pints/9 cups light stock or water

200g/7oz spring greens (collards) or kale, finely shredded

200g/7oz Chinese mustard cabbage, finely shredded

200g/7oz spinach, shredded

1 bunch of watercress, shredded

6 spring onions (scallions), shredded

25g/1oz/½ cup chopped fresh parsley

2.5ml/½ tsp ground allspice

¼ nutmeg, grated

a pinch of cayenne pepper

salt and freshly ground black pepper

French bread or garlic bread, to serve

1 Dice the ham quite small, keeping any fat and rind in one separate piece. Put the fat piece with the lard or oil into a deep pan and heat until it sizzles. Stir in the diced ham, onion, garlic, oregano and thyme and cook over a medium heat for 5 minutes, stirring occasionally.

2 Add the bay leaves, cloves, celery and green pepper and stir over a medium heat for another 2–3 minutes, then add the cabbage and stock or water. Bring to the boil and simmer gently for 5 minutes.

3 Add the spring greens or kale and mustard cabbage, boil for a further 2 minutes, then add the spinach, watercress and spring onions. Return to the boil, then lower the heat and simmer for 1 minute. Add the parsley, allspice and nutmeg, salt, black pepper and cayenne to taste.

4 Remove the piece of ham fat and, if you can find them, the cloves. Ladle into individual soup bowls and serve immediately, with warm French bread or garlic bread.

Galician Broth

This delicious main-meal soup is very similar to the warming, chunky meat and potato broths of cooler climates. For extra colour, a few onion skins can be added when cooking the gammon, but remove them before serving.

INGREDIENTS

Serves 4

450g/1lb piece gammon (cured ham)

2 bay leaves

2 onions, sliced

1.5 litres/2½ pints/6¼ cups cold water

10ml/2 tsp paprika

675g/1½ lb potatoes, cut into large chunks

225g/8oz spring greens (collards)

400g/14oz can haricot (navy) or cannellini
 beans, drained

salt and freshly ground black pepper

1 Soak the gammon overnight in cold water. Drain and put in a large pan with the bay leaves and onions. Pour the water on top.

2 Bring to the boil, then reduce the heat and simmer gently for about 1½ hours until the meat is tender. Keep an eye on the pan to make sure it doesn't boil over.

COOK'S TIP

Bacon knuckles can be used instead of the gammon (cured ham). The bones will give the juices a delicious flavour.

3 Drain the meat, reserving the cooking liquid, and leave to cool slightly. Discard the skin and any excess fat from the meat and cut into small chunks. Return to the pan with the paprika and potatoes. Cover and simmer gently for 20 minutes.

4 Cut away the cores from the greens. Roll up the leaves and cut into thin shreds. Add to the pan with the beans and simmer for about 10 minutes. Season with salt and freshly ground black pepper and serve piping hot.

Beef Noodle Soup

Offer your fortunate friends or family a steaming bowl of this soup, packed with delicious flavours of Asia.

INGREDIENTS

Serves 4

10g/¼oz dried porcini mushrooms

150ml/¼ pint/⅔ cup boiling water

6 spring onions (scallions)

115g/4oz carrots

350g/12oz rump (round) steak

about 30ml/2 tbsp oil

1 garlic clove, crushed

2.5cm/1in piece of fresh root ginger, peeled and finely chopped

1.2 litres/2 pints/5 cups beef stock

45ml/3 tbsp light soy sauce

60ml/4 tbsp dry sherry

75g/3oz thin egg noodles

75g/3oz spinach, shredded

salt and freshly ground black pepper

1 Break the mushrooms into small pieces, place in a bowl and pour over the boiling water. Leave to soak for 15 minutes.

2 Shred the spring onions and carrots into 5cm/2in long, fine strips. Trim any fat off the meat and slice into thin strips.

3 Heat the oil in a large pan and cook the beef, in batches, until browned, adding a little more oil if necessary. Remove the beef with a slotted spoon and drain thoroughly on kitchen paper.

4 Add the garlic, ginger, spring onions and carrots to the pan and stir-fry for 3 minutes.

5 Add the beef stock, the mushrooms and their soaking liquid, soy sauce and sherry. Season generously with salt and freshly ground black pepper. Bring to the boil and simmer, covered, for 10 minutes.

6 Break up the noodles slightly and add to the pan with the shredded spinach. Simmer gently for 5 minutes until the beef is tender. Adjust the seasoning to taste before serving.

COOK'S TIP

Dried porcini mushrooms are now widely available in supermarkets. They may seem expensive, but are full of flavour, so a small quantity goes a long way and really gives a lift to a soup like this one.

Index